Edward John Beale

English tobacco culture

being a description of the first English and Irish tobacco crops of 1886

Edward John Beale

English tobacco culture
being a description of the first English and Irish tobacco crops of 1886

ISBN/EAN: 9783744739870

Printed in Europe, USA, Canada, Australia, Japan

Cover: Foto ©ninafisch / pixelio.de

More available books at **www.hansebooks.com**

ENGLISH TOBACCO CULTURE

BEING A

Description of the First English and Irish Tobacco Crops of 1886.

WITH WHICH IS EMBODIED

A Paper

APPEARING IN THE

Journal of the Bath and West of England and Southern Counties Association.

EDITED BY

E. J. BEALE, F.L.S.,
Of the Firm of JAMES CARTER & CO.

WITH NUMEROUS ILLUSTRATIONS.

1887.

London:
E. MARLBOROUGH & CO.

[*All rights reserved.*]

DEDICATED,

BY ROYAL COMMAND,

TO

HER MOST GRACIOUS MAJESTY

QUEEN VICTORIA,

IN THE FIFTIETH (JUBILEE) YEAR OF HER MAJESTY'S REIGN,

BY

HER MAJESTY'S OBEDIENT SERVANT,

E. J. BEALE.

PREFACE.

THE condition of British agriculture has reached such a critical stage, that it is felt no apology is needed to introduce to the notice of the Farmer any new form of cultivation that may be thought to have a reasonable chance of success.

This being conceded, I feel justified in adding that last season's experiments in the cultivation of Tobacco, in England and Ireland, resulted in a degree satisfactory beyond the hopes of the most sanguine promoters of the experiments, and whilst I would most particularly desire to recommend the exercise of reasonable caution in the matter of the area or extent of future experiments, I feel that those results have more than justified further trials.

With historical precedents for its forcible exclusion, and with these prohibitions but imperfectly understood, it is not surprising that a certain amount of doubt and discouragement should have found expression; but I cannot agree with the opinion frequently expressed, that any great difficulty is to be feared in the thorough exercise of the Revenue regulations; and I venture to repeat here a simple Form of License that I have already suggested to Her Majesty's Government, believing that a license something in the way of my plan would meet all the requirements of the Board of Inland Revenue, and would moreover present the subject to the eye of the British Farmer in a far more popular form than is obtained by the cumbersome system of sureties at present demanded by the authorities before the cultivation of a Tobacco crop is sanctioned.

Full Name and Address of Cultivator.	Name of Parish in which Crop is to be grown.	Name and Address of Owner of Land where Crop is to be grown.	Name and Address of Tenant of the Land on which Crop is to be grown.	Name by which Field is identified by the Occupier.	Acreage intended to be grown.	Variety intended to be grown.

LICENSE TO GROW TOBACCO UNDER EXCISE REGULATIONS.

This Form to be obtainable, for a fee of one shilling, by any one desirous of cultivating a larger area of Tobacco than the law allows to be grown free of duty. Such a License, we presume, would be in duplicate; the one retained by the authorities would contain full particulars of the locality in which the crop was intended to be produced. By this means the Government will have at their fingerends a complete list that can be readily divided out and placed in the hands of the various Excise officers in the country, whilst the penalties already existing under statute, promptly enforced from any one cultivating an acreage Tobacco crop without being in possession of this License, would very soon make things comfortable all round.

The reader will observe that it has only been possible to give an approximate estimate of the average weight per acre of cured Tobacco of the following varieties, i.e., "One Sucker," "Big Frederick," "Connecticut Seedleaf," "Havana," and "Island Broadleaf," from the fact that the workpeople had begun to pack them down before weighing was suggested. In all other cases the weights are actually correct.

Up to the period of the publication of this work, there was not in existence any Guide Book or recognised code of instruction for the use of experimentalists. "English Tobacco Culture" is anticipated to supply that want; and I have every reason to hope that the thorough observations and records made by the various noblemen and gentlemen whose experiences are recorded here, will furnish sufficient information to guide the cultivator, and supply a want that is deemed of urgent importance.

E. J. BEALE.

January, 1887.

CONTENTS.

	PAGE
INTRODUCTION . . .	1
THE HISTORY OF TOBACCO . . .	11
SNUFF-TAKING .	18
A CONCISE DIARY ON AVERAGE OPERATIONS IN TOBACCO CULTURE	19
THE PRINCIPAL VARIETIES OF TOBACCO CULTIVATED IN ENGLAND AND IRELAND IN 1886 .	21
DESCRIPTIONS AND ILLUSTRATIONS OF SEVENTEEN VARIETIES OF TOBACCO	24
DESCRIPTION OF THE CULTIVATION OF MESSRS. CARTERS' TOBACCO CROP . .	58
HARVESTING MESSRS. CARTERS' TOBACCO CROP .	64
CURING MESSRS. CARTERS' TOBACCO	67

CONTENTS.

	PAGE
"HANDING" AND FINISHING MESSRS. CARTERS' TOBACCO FOR MARKET	72
CONTINENTAL TOBACCO CULTURE	79
GROWTH OF TOBACCO BY LORD WALSINGHAM	83
,, ,, SIR EDWARD BIRKBECK	86
,, ,, FAUNCE DE LAUNE, ESQ.	89
,, ,, C. J. WALLACE, ESQ., IN IRELAND	92
,, ,, L. M'CORMICK, ESQ. ,,	94
THE CULTIVATION OF TOBACCO IN STOCKHOLM	97
THE TOBACCO WORM	100
A USEFUL TOBACCO BARN	103
ENGLISH TOBACCO CULTURE A HUNDRED YEARS AGO	104
TOBACCO IN NEW ZEALAND, GERMANY, FRANCE, AMERICA, AUSTRALIA, SPAIN, ETC.	113
USEFUL HINTS CULLED FROM THE BRAINS OF AMERICAN CULTIVATORS	118

ILLUSTRATIONS.

		PAGE
TOBACCO—KENTUCKY		24
,,	YELLOW PRIOR	26
,,	WHITE BURLEIGH	28
,,	ORINOCO	30
,,	GLASNER	32
,,	FLORIDA	34
,,	VIRGINIA	36
,,	MARYLAND BROADLEAF	38
,,	CONNECTICUT	40
,,	WHITE STEM	42
,,	PENNSYLVANIA	44
,,	HESTER VIRGINIA	46
,,	ISLAND BROADLEAF	48
,,	ONE SUCKER	50
,,	BIG FREDERICK	52
,,	CONNECTICUT SEEDLEAF	54
"PICKING-UP" MESSRS. CARTERS' GREEN CROP OF TOBACCO		64
SECTION SHOWING INTERIOR OF BARN USED IN CURING MESSRS. CARTERS' TOBACCO		65
CARTERS' TOBACCO FURNACE		70
STRIPPING AND HANDING MESSRS. CARTERS' TOBACCO		73
THE TOBACCO WORM		100
A USEFUL TOBACCO BARN		103

ENGLISH TOBACCO CULTURE.

INTRODUCTION.

THE question of the successful cultivation of Tobacco in Great Britain has created an amount of interest amongst agriculturists that its originators can scarcely have foreseen; in fact, this subject is undoubtedly the most important of the many panaceas that have been suggested for the amelioration of the present depressed condition of British agriculture; whilst there is, probably, no other innovation that has met with a similar amount of hostile criticism, not only from the pens of agriculturists, scientists, and pessimists, but also from numerous manufacturers and others more or less professionally interested in the product.

The origin of the movement is stated by Mr. Kains-Jackson (in an excellent article entitled "Tobacco at Home," published in "The

Farmers' Almanack" for 1887), to have commenced with some remarks made by Mr. de Laune at an agricultural meeting when reviewing the existing depression of the farming interests. At any rate, the subject was brought prominently into notice on the 29th day of March last year (1886) by Lord Harris—a neighbour of Mr. de Laune—in a practical and powerful speech in the House of Lords; and although their lordships did not arrive at any determination, it was generally admitted that the importance of the question justified the fullest inquiry, and hopes were freely expressed by both branches of the Legislature that experiments might be made with a view to determine whether Tobacco could be depended upon as a farm crop in Great Britain; and if so, could it be cultivated to give a reasonable profit to the producer? As the result of a discussion in the Lower House, the Government suggested that the Council of the Royal Agricultural Society should lend its powerful aid in assisting the experiments, and at a meeting of the Council on the 6th of April, under the presidency of H.R.H. The Prince of Wales, the subject of Tobacco-growing was discussed at considerable length; but no practical action was taken by the Society—on the contrary, an opinion was expressed that the season was too far advanced to hope for any chance of success, and, so far as the Royal Agricultural Society's interest extended at that time, the matter lapsed. The severe restrictions considered necessary by the Board of Inland Revenue doubtless also induced many who were disposed to encourage and assist the experiment, to give up the idea.

In the meantime, recognising the necessity for prompt action if the season was to be saved, Messrs. Carter cabled to America and from the most reliable sources obtained seeds of those varieties of Tobacco that from the locality of their introduction were considered best adapted to the English climate. At this early period, Messrs. Carter, at the suggestion of Mr. Kains-Jackson and others, had determined to make an experiment in the growth of Tobacco as a farmer's crop at their own expense, the intention being at that time to establish the fact whether Tobacco could or could not be *successfully grown* in this country; and —bearing in mind the prohibitory Excise conditions—to destroy the Tobacco upon the ground after the question of the possibility of *successfully growing* the crop had been fully established.

Several noblemen, landowners, and agriculturists also obtained plants or seeds from Messrs. Carter, amongst others, Lord Walsingham in

Norfolk, Mr. Faunce de Laune in Kent, and Mr. Bateman in Essex, and the crops grown upon the estates of these gentlemen (with that of Messrs. Carter) formed the principal average experiments of the year, although less important experiments were made in Berkshire, Devon, Worcestershire, Westmoreland, etc.

Lord Walsingham's crop (more fully described at page 83) consisted of the "Pennsylvania," "Big Frederick," "Virginia," and "Connecticut" (the three first-named being varieties of a high standard of excellence), and was planted in a somewhat exposed situation having an eastern aspect, yet the results, so far as the growth of the crop was concerned, are reported as being most satisfactory; and sanguine hopes may reasonably be entertained as to the ultimate success of his lordship's experiments, which can only be fully determined after the Tobacco has passed into the hands of the manufacturer.

Mr. Bateman's crop in Essex and Mr. de Laune's acreage in Kent were marvellous examples of what high farming with the advantage of favourable surroundings will accomplish, and it is to be regretted that by an unfortunate accident the value of Mr. Bateman's experiment was lost, the Tobacco being destroyed by fire during the process of curing.

Mr. de Laune's crop was grown under conditions of an exceptionally favourable nature for the development of the plant, the Tobacco being planted in small sections, these in their turn margined with hops. Unquestionably, the protection afforded by the hops tended to concentrate and retain the sun heat, with the result that the plants reached an enormous size, prodigious leaves being produced that would astonish cultivators in many other countries; but at the same time it is questionable whether these conditions of cultivation were desirable.

An opinion has been expressed that these circumstances were not the most acceptable, inasmuch as whilst Messrs. Carters' plants, exposed more or less to the action of the air and wind on all sides, and planted very wide apart, were fast ripening when the crop was harvested, Mr. de Laune's plants—put into the ground at the same time—had the appearance of being still in growth, or at any rate (except in the case of the "Kentucky"—an unusually early kind) the leaves were quite green and full of sap when seen upon the land some days after the whole of Messrs. Carters' crop had been housed.

A recent Government inquiry into the growth of Tobacco in the United States shows that while the Tobacco plant exhibits a great facility in adapting itself to various soils and climates, its cultivation is practically restricted to 16 States. In the last census year the total crop produced was 472,661,158 lbs., and of this the 16 Tobacco-growing States produced 469,816,203 lbs. For the whole of the United States the average crop per acre was 740 lbs., but it may be taken that for the 16 Tobacco-growing States, the average was about 1,500 lbs. per acre, the variation being from 900 to about 2,000 lbs.

In compiling this work endeavours have been made to confine the main body of remarks to the English experiments, and to abstain from referring (except in notable instances) either to the locality in which Tobacco is produced in other countries or to the various forms of cultivation practised, and with which many are more or less familiar, failing to see what good results can accrue from such comparison; and it is difficult to determine the practical value that can be claimed for the lengthy paper upon the subject of "The Cultivation of Tobacco in the North-West of Europe," published in Part 2, Vol. 22, of the Royal Agricultural Society's Journal, inasmuch as the notes in question are almost entirely devoted to foreign cultivation, and embody to a very large extent the opinions of cultivators in climates very different from that of England. English farmers can have nothing to do with foreign producers of Tobacco. The fact remains that something like 50 millions of pounds of Tobacco are annually consumed in this country; and the question to solve is—" Shall we grow it ourselves, or buy it from the foreigners?"

Mr. Kains-Jackson writes as follows in "The Farmers' Almanack" for 1887:

"For half a century nearly the illustrations given of current events have never included amongst the products of an English harvest a crop of Tobacco. It was reserved for 1886 to see the plant cultivated and dried in Great Britain as a farm crop.

"Our English growers have this encouragement: that English soil and climate have, undoubtedly, produced Tobacco plants of astonishing luxuriance, and that whatever failure ensues—and failure in several respects is not likely to be avoided this first season—will carry with it its own explanation and cure.

"Like many other things, the English climate has proved not so bad as report made it. What was said to be impossible, the rearing and maturing the Tobacco plant in England, has been accomplished, and this season's results are thought as not unlikely to be the beginning of a new and great industry in the United Kingdom.

"Line upon line instructions accumulate 'how to do it,' so that now it may be feared, from the multiplication of advisers, the experimentalists will hesitate and be lost. Lucky will be the grower who has the aid of a practical expert, although but a common labourer in a Tobacco plantation, who would know the mature from the immature leaf, have it timely gathered and dried through its scale of degrees in temperature, in a suitable building. A fair field and no favour is all that our little Tobacco harvest requires."

The following are extracts from Lord Harris's speech in the House of Lords: "Sir John Sinclair, in his General Report of Scotland, says: 'During the American war this article (Tobacco) became so dear that several unsuccessful attempts were made in Scotland for its cultivation. The chief seat of that new culture was in the neighbourhood of Kelso,' where 'it succeeded so well that 16½ statute acres of Crailing brought £104, or £6 7s. 4d. per acre, being purchased by the Government at 4d. per pound.' From the agricultural survey of the county of Roxburgh, dated 1794, it appeared that 'Tobacco was first grown at Newstead, and eventually many hundred acres of land were cropped with it. The profits were amazingly great, but an Act of Parliament put an entire stop to its cultivation.' Mr. Train also gave evidence that land let for Tobacco cultivation used to let at £5 an acre, when other land was only fetching £2. A more extensive experiment was made in the Vale of York for a few years before 1782, which had to be abandoned because the penalties laid amounted to £30,000. In Ireland the duty was removed in 1822, but was re-imposed about 1830. By 1829 or 1830 there were no fewer than 1,000 acres under Tobacco cultivation in Ireland. It might be questionable whether if cultivated in this country Tobacco would bear a duty of 3s. 6d. a pound, but it must be remembered that we were rapidly becoming accustomed to a much smaller margin of profit than was required by our forefathers. The following amusing extract from Fairholt proves the advantages which had formerly accrued from the cultivation of Tobacco in England:

"'It had been extensively grown in Gloucestershire, as appears from the following passage in "Harry Hangman's Honour, or the Glostershire Hangman's request to the Smokers and Tobacconists of London," a quarto pamphlet in the King's Collection, June 11, 1655. He says: "The very planting of Tobacco hath proved the decay of my trade, for since it hath been planted in Glostershire, especially at Winchcourt, my trade has proved nothing worth." He adds: "Then 'twas a merry world with me! for indeed before Tobacco was there planted there being no kind of trade to employ men, and very small tillage, necessity compelled poor men to stand my friends by stealing of sheep and other cattel, breaking of hedges, robbing of orchards, and what not."'

"In Belgium, an ordinary year yielded 2,700 lbs. of Tobacco an English acre, of which 70 per cent. was first quality and 30 per cent. second and third quality. The first quality sold at $6\frac{1}{2}$d. per lb., and the second and third at about $4\frac{1}{2}$d. The net profit was about £26 an acre. The industry had made the fortune of the frontier town of Blandain, and enabled it successfully to tide over the present agricultural crisis."

> *When all things were made,*
> *None was made better than Tobacco,*
> *To be a lone man's companion, a bachelor's friend*
> *A hungry man's food, a sad man's cordial,*
> *A wakeful man's sleep, and a chilly man's fire.*
> *There's no herb like it under the canopy of Heaven.*
>
> C. KINGSLEY.

THE HISTORY OF TOBACCO.

HISTORIANS are not in harmony as to the origin of Tobacco, and it is impossible to satisfactorily fix the period at which it was first introduced into England, or by whom its introduction was accomplished. Some writers assert that the first plants of Tobacco were discovered in the province of Yucatan—a Spanish possession—under the name of "petum," about the year 1520. Thence it found its way to North America, the West Indies, Spain, and Portugal, and subsequently into France at the hands of one Jean Nicot, whose surname has served as the base for the scientific term "Nicotiana," now universally adopted.

Mr. Philip Meadows Taylor, in his work, "Tobacco—A Farmer's Crop," says: "It appears certain that Fernandez Cortez observed the Tobacco plant in 1519, when he invaded Mexico. Whilst other Historians state that Tobacco was known to the Spaniards in Cuba as far back as 1492."

Mr. Meadows Taylor states that Tobacco was known as "Yoli," or "Petun," by the North American Indians.

Sir Walter Raleigh is generally credited with having brought Tobacco from Virginia to England about the year 1586, and it is stated that at that early period large tracts of Tobacco were annually under cultivation in Portugal.

An amusing anecdote (recorded in an old volume referring to Tobacco) is related of Sir Walter Raleigh.

It is said that having one day retired to his room to smoke, after the manner of the inhabitants of Virginia, he ordered his servant to bring him a cup of beer. The servant on bringing the beer was surprised to see what he had never seen before, and dashing the liquid in Sir Walter Raleigh's face he ran down the stairs, crying out *that his master's head was on fire, and that the smoke was coming out of both his mouth and nostrils.*

The origin of the popular name of "Tobacco" is as uncertain as that of the period of its introduction. Some authorities assert that it is derived from Tobago, an island on the West Indies; Humboldt states that the word Tobacco is a remnant of the ancient Haytian language, and that the name denotes the tube through which the smoke is inhaled by the smoker; some writers state that the word takes its origin from Tobacco, in Mexico; whilst others again declare that the word owes its origin to Tabac—the name of an instrument used by native Americans in the preparation of the herb; others, again, declaring that Tobacco was called by the Aztecs "Yetl."

Tobacco has thus been in use in England for at least 350 years, and Du Tour claims for it, "that it gives pleasure to the savage and philosopher alike—whether on the burning desert or at the frozen zone."

It is stated that a hundred volumes had been written against the practice of smoking by the beginning of the eighteenth century, whilst at Constantinople any Turk found smoking was led through the streets with a pipe thrust through his nose. One of the Turkish Sultans (Amurath IV.) rendered smoking a capital offence. In our own land James I. endeavoured, both by the means of a book written by His Majesty and by severe penalties, to suppress the use of Tobacco, but without success.

The following amusing poem is given in an old volume treating upon "Tobacco":

"ON A PIPE OF TOBACCO."

Pretty tube of mighty power!
Charmer of an idle hour;
Object of my hot desire,
Lip of wax and eye of fire;
And thy snowy taper waist,
With my fingers gently braced;
And thy lovely swelling crest,
With my bended stopper prest;
And the sweetest bliss of blisses,
Breathing from thy balmy kisses;
Happy thrice, and thrice again—
Happiest he of happy men;
Who, when the night again returns,
When again the taper burns,
When again the cricket gay,
(Little crickets, full of play)
Can afford his tube to feed
With the fragrant Indian weed,
Pleasure for a nose divine,
Incense of the god of wine;
Happy thrice, and thrice again—
Happiest he of happy men!

Tobacco cultivation is no new institution in Europe, for as far back as 1830 it was grown in Russia, Holland, Denmark, Germany, Italy, France, Sicily, and Turkey, as well as in India, Persia, Syria, Arabia, and other more Eastern latitudes.

A well-informed writer, about the beginning of the eighteenth century,* says: "Tobacco can be readily raised in almost all the temperate climates of the globe; and the chief reason why it is not better known to the English cultivator is, that we have laws which prohibit its culture under severe penalties. The cultivation of Tobacco in England was finally prohibited by law in 1782." The same

* "A Practical Treatise on the History and Medical Properties and Cultivation of Tobacco," by James Jennings. 1830.

writer adds that, "Several tons of Irish-grown Tobacco was imported into England about this time at a duty of 2s. a lb., whilst that imported from America paid 3s. a lb. duty."

The following is a summary of the Laws which prohibited the growth of Tobacco in this country fifty years since, and which, with the later enactments under George III. and William IV., govern the existing prohibitions:

> By Charles II., c. 34, no person shall plant any Tobacco on pain of forfeiting the same, or the value thereof, or 40s. for every rod or pole of ground planted with it (equivalent to a duty of £320 per acre); half to the King and half to him who sues. And besides the said penalty by 15 Charles II., c. 7, he shall moreover forfeit £10 for every rod or pole; one-third to the King, one-third to the poor, and one-third to him who sues.
>
> By 22 and 23 of Charles II., c. 26, the justices shall, a month before every sessions, issue their warrants to all high and petty constables to search what Tobacco is planted, cured, and made, and by whom; and to make presentment of such persons; which presentment shall be filed by the Clerk of the Peace in open sessions; such filing to be a sufficient conviction of the persons presented, unless such person having notice given him of such presentment, shall, at the next sessions, traverse the presentment, and find sureties for prosecuting and trying such traverse.
>
> And all constables, etc., shall, within fourteen days after warrant from two justices, pluck up, burn, consume, or tear in pieces, and utterly destroy all

Tobacco, seed, plant, and leaf sowed or growing in any field or ground.

And if any Tobacco shall be suffered to grow or be consumed in seed, plant, or leaf by the space of fourteen days after the receipt of such warrant by the constables or other officers, they shall for every offence forfeit 5s. for every rod, pole, or perch planted with Tobacco; half to the King and half to him who sues.

But, by the several Acts, nothing in them is to hinder planting Tobacco in gardens for physic or surgery, so that the quantity planted exceed not half a pole of ground.

These penalties failing to stop the cultivation of the plant another Act was passed. By 15th Charles II., cap. vii., sections 15, 16, and 17, the tax of £320 was raised to £1,600 per acre, and that exists to the present day.

The cultivation of Tobacco in England was first prohibited during the Commonwealth, and as an anecdote connected with this subject, it may be mentioned that Oliver Cromwell ordered upon one occasion, a troop of horse to enter into a field and trample down a Tobacco plantation; of so much consequence while we had Colonies, was the trade with such Colonies esteemed. Now, however, as the North American States have been long since an independent Government, there appears no substantial reason for such laws as the preceding continuing in existence.

Adam Smith, in his "Wealth of Nations" (Book I. chapter xi.), says: "Tobacco *might be* cultivated with advantage through the greater part of Europe, but in almost every part of Europe it has become a principal subject of taxation, and to collect a tax from every different farm in the country where this plant might happen to be cultivated, would be more difficult, *it has been supposed*, than to levy one upon its importation at the Custom House. *The cultivation of Tobacco has upon this account been most absurdly* prohibited through the greater part of Europe, which necessarily gives a sort of monopoly to the countries where *it is* allowed."

That excuses have been allowed from time to time for the cultivation of Tobacco on an extended scale is shown by the following paragraph from Marshall's Reports to the Board of Agriculture (1815): "Of Tobacco a considerable patch was cultivated at Rothwell, in Northamptonshire, in 1806, for the purpose of dressing sheep for the scab."

With respect to the risks of cultivators evading the Excise, Mr. Meadows Taylor, in his excellent treatise already referred to, when describing the French system of cultivation says: "Our wary Gascon peasant is far too wide awake to run the risk of the loss of his licence, joined to a ruinous fine, for the sake of pilfering a few pounds of bad, unsaleable Tobacco. I say unsaleable, because the peasant would first have much difficulty in obtaining in secret good dried leaf, and then to convert this into smoking Tobacco, the process of fermentation is only to be properly got through by operating on large quantities."

SNUFF-TAKING:

ITS ORIGIN, Etc.

About the year 1700 the practice of taking Snuff was entirely confined to foreigners resident in England, and to a few English gentlemen who had acquired the habit during a sojourn abroad; but shortly after that date, Sir George Rooke, when in command of the British Fleet, made a descent upon Cadiz, where he captured amongst various other prizes several thousand barrels of fine Snuff. That portion of the Snuff that found its way to England was sold by the waggon-load in Portsmouth, Chatham, Plymouth, and other ports at 3d. and 4d. a pound. From this distribution is dated the general habit of Snuff-taking in England.

A CONCISE DIARY
ON
AVERAGE OPERATIONS IN TOBACCO CULTURE,

BASED UPON MESSRS. CARTERS' EXPERIMENTS, 1886.

Autumn & Winter Preparation. THE land should be, if possible, Autumn ploughed, and then left for the winter, to have the benefit of the frost upon the soil.

Early Spring. A second ploughing will be found beneficial, to be repeated if the soil is of a tenacious character; the well-rotted manure being worked in at the same time.

March 1st (about). Make a first sowing of Tobacco seed, mixed with ten times its bulk of ashes or fine soil, in a manure bed, or in pans, in a heated frame, being careful not to bury the seed—all that is necessary is to scatter it over the surface, and then to press firmly, following by liberal watering with a rose pot. When plants are up and look established, take every opportunity of giving air as freely as possible, even to removing the covering altogether when weather permits.

April 1st. Make a second sowing of Tobacco seed in case of accident to the first sowing, or in view of a late spring.

April 15th to May 1st (about). Transplant the seedlings into small boxes—say twenty inches long, fourteen inches wide, and three inches deep—each of these boxes should hold about twenty-four plants; keep them close for two or three days and shade from direct sun, then gradually remove covering and give all air and light possible, the object being to harden off the plants and prepare them for the field.

June 1st (about). Plant out the Tobacco on the ridges as described at page 59, and setting the plants thus— three feet apart in the row, and making the ridges three feet apart from each other.

Plant towards latter part of the day, and in showery, dull weather, if possible. In the absence of rain, water freely as soon as planted.

July 1st (about). Keep down weeds by horse-hoeing.

July 15th (about). Earth up Tobacco—*i.e.*, with the hands or a small hoe, draw up the loose earth cut aside from the ridges by the horse-hoe, around the plant into the form of an ant-hill or a round hillock.

August 1st (about). Watch for appearance of flower-stem, which must be pinched out with the thumb and finger as soon as it is visible. Keep down weeds.

Aug. 15th. Look out for suckers which grow out from the junction of the leaf and main stem, removing them as soon as they appear.

Sept. 1st. Get barn or house ready in which Tobacco is to be cured.

The crop (according to the season and locality) should be nearly ready to harvest now (*see page* 64).

Sept. 15th. Assuming that the crop has just been cut and housed (*see pages* 64–66), if the weather is bright and the air dry give as much light and air as possible by day, carefully closing up at night.

Sept. 20th. Commence artificial drying by stove (*see page* 70), or similar appliance, if available. Exclude damp, fog, etc.; commence firing at a temperature of about fifty degrees and gradually advance to ninety degrees. The duration of "firing" at this high temperature cannot be indicated here, but must be left largely to the good sense of the operator—always remembering that it is better to cure slowly rather than fast.

THE VARIETIES OF TOBACCO CULTIVATED IN ENGLAND AND IRELAND IN 1886,

BY

Lord Walsingham, Mr. Faunce de Laune, Mr. Bateman, Messrs. Carter, and others,

FROM SEEDS SUPPLIED BY

James Carter & Co.

With the object of determining whether any variety of Tobacco was the better adapted to our climate, Messrs. Carter decided to plant a given quantity of each of the seventeen sorts of which they had imported seeds. Of these, two gave evidence of apparently being too delicate to withstand the effects of our uncertain English summer, i.e., the "Kentucky" and the "White Burleigh," inasmuch that the plants appeared to ripen off before the full growth was reached; this was especially apparent upon the wet portion of the land. The appearance of these varieties led some writers to assume that their cultivation was a failure, but after experience did not tend to indorse that opinion, and it is necessary to wait until the Tobacco is manufactured, when the relative values of the different kinds will be ascertained. It is, however, admitted that the early maturity of " White Burleigh " and " Kentucky" is a natural result, and these two varieties will unquestionably become favourites with many future cultivators desirous of producing colour rather than quantity, especially in instances where the soil is of a warm character, or in protected situations, the beautiful golden hue of the dried leaf having been pronounced by several authorities equal to anything that can be produced elsewhere.

A further result of this extended trial of varieties has resulted in Messrs. Carter being able to divide the Tobaccos into two sections, an arrangement that will doubtless be found acceptable for the future guidance of cultivators.

The one section is well represented by the " Kentucky," and may be described as semi-erect leaved, the main stem of the plant being more or less hidden by the pale green foliage (*see Illustration No.* 1, *page* 24).

The opposite section is composed of those

varieties having pendant leaves, and described in the following pages as "horizontal-leaved," the surface of all of which become more or less corrugated as the plants mature, the colour of the leaves being of a deep green, with the main stem very prominent. Of these the variety known as "Big Frederick" (see *Illustration* No. 15, *page* 52) may be taken as a good type. The relative qualities of the leaves are also governed by this selection, those of the latter section being of considerably greater substance or more "leathery" in texture than the "Kentucky."

TOBACCO—VAR. KENTUCKY.
Grown in MESSRS. CARTERS' FIELD CROP, 1886.
Photographed on Wood.

TOBACCO—KENTUCKY.
(Semi-erect leaved.)

This variety, in conjunction with the "White Burleigh" (see page 29), has attained greater prominence in the public mind than any other kind, inasmuch as in the earlier stages of growth the peculiar lemon yellow colour of the leaves was attributed to a want of constitution in the plant. It *is one of the earliest* Tobaccos that can be grown in this country.

In this variety perhaps more than in any other, the semi-erect habit of the upper leaves is retained even when the flower-stem is thrown out—as shown in the opposite Illustration. The leaves are very long, tapering, and with an even upper surface which is maintained throughout its growth. Midrib rather broad and of a bright creamy lemon colour, the lesser ribs faintly developed and of a slightly deeper colour than the midrib. Colour of flowers— rich rose.

The short main stem is hidden by the upper leaves, distance between the leaves about an inch, with eleven to thirteen leaves upon a plant.

Average height of plant when topped (Sept. 15)	38½ inches.
Average length of largest leaves	27¼ ,,
Average width of largest leaves	13 ,,

𝔈𝔰𝔱𝔦𝔪𝔞𝔱𝔢𝔡 𝔅𝔞𝔩𝔞𝔫𝔠𝔢 𝔖𝔥𝔢𝔢𝔱.

Showing cost of production, and average value of a crop of one acre of Kentucky. The value of the produce of this variety being calculated upon the weight of 66 plants, as grown by Messrs. Carter, including all leaves, good, bad, and indifferent, which, when stripped from the stalks and cured, actually weighed 32 pounds, or equal to about 2,100 pounds per acre, allowing 4,840 plants per acre.

	£ s. d.	£ s. d.
By Produce of Tobacco cured ready for sale to manufacturer, say 2,400 lbs. @ 4d.*		40 0 0
To Rent of Land and Buildings, including Rates, Tithes, and Taxes, @ 60/- per acre	£3 0 0	
3 Ploughings @ 10/- per acre each time	1 10 0	
2 Harrowings @ 1/- per acre each time	0 2 0	
9 Loads Farm-yard Manure delivered on Land	2 8 0	
Spreading Farm-yard Manure	0 1 3	
3 cwt. Peruvian Guano @ £12 per ton	1 16 0	
5,000 Plants at about 15/- per 1,000	3 15 0	
Planting ditto, 1 man 1 day 3/2, 1 boy 1 day 1/3	0 4 5	
2 Horse-hoeings @ 3/- per acre each time	0 6 0	
Manual labour, hiling and side-hoeing twice over @ 7/- per acre each time	0 14 0	
Pruning, topping, and suckering @ 8/- per acre	0 8 0	
Cutting @ 5/- per acre, carting to barn and hanging @ 12/-	0 17 0	
Firing, 2 loads waste hard wood to be found on the Farm (charge for labour only)	0 16 0	
Man's time curing and attending, etc., 2 weeks @ 15/-	1 10 0	
Stripping, sorting, bulking, and packing, say 2,400 lbs. @ 5/- per 100 lbs.	6 0 0	23 7 8
Average profit upon 1 acre		£16 12 4

* It is considered that 4d. per lb. *is the lowest value at which average quality Tobacco can reasonably be placed.*

TOBACCO—VAR. YELLOW PRIOR.
Grown in MESSRS. CARTERS' FIELD CROP, 1886.
Photographed on Wood.

TOBACCO—YELLOW PRIOR.
(Horizontal leaved.)

PROBABLY one of the finest and best-looking Tobaccos of the entire Group. It may be classed as *second early*, and it undoubtedly possesses a strong constitution that recommends its trial on a more extended area.

As shown in the Illustration opposite, the leaves are very large—somewhat less pointed than others—of very great substance, and deeply corrugated and gummy in a mature state. This variety also ripens early, as shown by the colouring of the outer portions of the leaves. The midrib is deep green; the lesser ribs, or veins, being very pronounced, and of a pale creamy yellow colour. Colour of flowers, rosy mauve.

The main stem is of a distinct deep green colour, immensely thick and of very stout texture. Average distance between leaves, 2 to 2½ inches; nine to twelve leaves being the number left upon each plant after being "topped."

Average height of plant when topped (Sept. 15) 46 inches.
Average length of largest leaves   ..   „   27   „
Average width of largest leaves   ..   „   14¾   „

Estimated Balance Sheet.

Showing cost of production, and average value of a crop of one acre of Yellow Prior. The value of the produce of this variety being calculated upon the weight of 18 plants, as grown by Messrs. Carter, including all leaves, good, bad, and indifferent, which, when stripped from the stalks and cured, actually weighed 9 pounds, or equal to about 2,420 pounds per acre, allowing 4,840 plants per acre.

		£	s.	d.
By Produce of Tobacco cured ready for sale to manufacturer, say 2,420 lbs. @ 4d.*		40	6	8
To Rent of Land and Buildings, including Rates, Tithes, and Taxes, @ 60/- per acre .. £3 0 0				
3 Ploughings @ 10/- per acre each time .. 1 10 0				
2 Harrowings @ 1/- per acre each time .. 0 2 0				
9 Loads Farm-yard Manure delivered on Land .. 2 8 0				
Spreading Farm-yard Manure .. 0 1 3				
3 cwt. Peruvian Guano @ £12 per ton .. 1 16 0				
5,000 Plants at about 15/- per 1,000 .. 3 15 0				
Planting ditto, 1 man 1 day 3/2, 1 boy 1 day 1/3 .. 0 4 5				
2 Horse-hoeings @ 3/- per acre each time .. 0 6 0				
Manual labour, billing and side-hoeing twice over @ 7/- per acre each time .. 0 14 0				
Pruning, topping, and suckering @ 8/- per acre .. 0 8 0				
Cutting @ 5/- per acre, carting to barn and hanging @ 12/- 0 17 0				
Firing, 2 loads waste hard wood to be found on the Farm (charge for labour only) .. 0 16 0				
Man's time curing and attending, etc., 2 weeks @ 15/- 1 10 0				
Stripping, sorting, bulking, and packing, say 2,420 lbs. @ 5/- per 100 lbs. .. 6 1 0		23	8	8
Average profit upon 1 acre ..		£16	18	0

* It is considered that 4d. per lb. *is the lowest value at which average quality Tobacco can reasonably be placed.*

TOBACCO—VAR. WHITE BURLEIGH.
Grown in MESSRS. CARTERS' FIELD CROP, 1886.
Photographed on Wood.

TOBACCO—WHITE BURLEIGH.
(Semi-erect leaved.)

This handsome *first early* variety is faithfully represented by the opposite Illustration, and the peculiar colour of the plants in growth gave rise to considerable discussion as to whether it was sufficiently hardy to stand the vicissitudes of an English climate. That such a result was realised is indisputable, and there is no doubt but that the "White Burleigh" and the "Kentucky" will be popular varieties in the future, especially where colour rather than quantity is aimed at.

As with the "Kentucky" the erect habit of the upper foliage is retained, even after the flower-stem is thrown out. The leaves are long, broad, tapering, of a yellowish green colour, and very gummy; midrib nearly white, lesser ribs or veins creamy white and prominent, surface fairly even at all stages of growth. Colour of flowers, pale rose.

Again, like the "Kentucky,' the short stout main stem is entirely hidden by the upper leaves, which are placed about an inch apart—there being an average of from ten to thirteen leaves upon each plant after being topped.

Average height of plant when topped (Sept. 15) 34 inches.
Average length of largest leaves ,, 27 ,,
Average width of largest leaves ,, 12½ ,,

Estimated Balance Sheet.

Showing cost of production, and average value of a crop of one acre of White Burleigh. The value of the produce of this variety being calculated upon the weight of 72 plants, as grown by Messrs. Carter, including all leaves, good, bad, and indifferent, which, when stripped from the stalks and cured, actually weighed 24 pounds, or equal to about 1,610 pounds per acre, allowing 4,840 plants per acre.

	£ s. d.	£ s. d.
By Produce of Tobacco cured ready for sale to manufacturer, say 1,610 lbs. @ 4d.*		26 16 8
To Rent of Land and Buildings, including Rates, Tithes, and Taxes, @ 60/- per acre	£3 0 0	
3 Ploughings @ 10/- per acre each time	1 10 0	
2 Harrowings @ 1/- per acre each time	0 2 0	
9 Loads Farm-yard Manure delivered on Land	2 8 0	
Spreading Farm-yard Manure	0 1 3	
3 cwt. Peruvian Guano @ £12 per ton	1 16 0	
5,000 Plants at about 15 - per 1,000	3 15 0	
Planting ditto, 1 man 1 day 3/2, 1 boy 1 day 1/3	0 4 5	
2 Horse-hoeings @ 3/- per acre each time	0 6 0	
Manual labour, hilling and side-hoeing twice over @ 7/- per acre each time	0 14 0	
Pruning, topping, and suckering @ 8/- per acre	0 8 0	
Cutting @ 5/- per acre, carting to barn and hanging @ 12/-	0 17 0	
Firing, 2 loads waste hard wood to be found on the Farm (charge for labour only)	0 16 0	
Man's time curing and attending, etc., 2 weeks @ 15/-	1 10 0	
Stripping, sorting, bulking, and packing, say 1,610 lbs. @ 5/- per 100 lbs.	4 0 6	21 8 2
Average profit upon 1 acre		£5 8 6

* It is considered that 4d. per lb. *is the lowest value at which average quality Tobacco can reasonably be placed.*

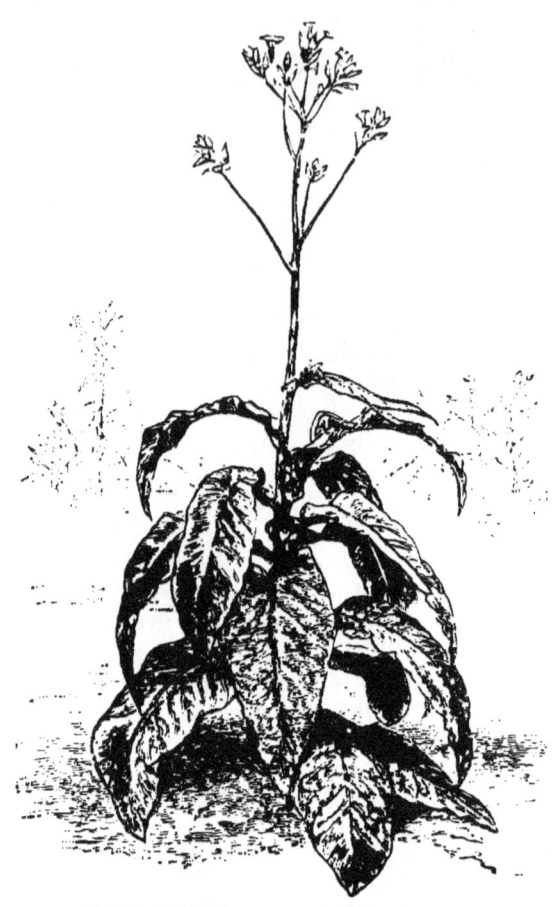

TOBACCO—VAR. ORINOCO.
Grown in Messrs. Carters' Field Crop, 1886.
Photographed on Wood.

TOBACCO—YELLOW ORINOCO.
(Horizontal leaved.)

This proves to be a *first early variety* of considerable excellence.

The size and beauty of the foliage are well shown in the opposite Illustration.

The leaves are of medium length and of a rich green colour —deeply corrugated as they approach maturity—and less tapering in form than some other kinds. As with "Big Frederick," the outer edges of the leaves show indications of ripening upon the plant at an early period. Midrib bright green, with lesser ribs or veins fairly prominent. Colour of flowers, salmon rose.

The main stem is very stout and hard, and the leaves have the peculiar leathery touch so much approved by the numerous experts who have inspected the English crops. Average distance between leaves, 2 inches; nine to twelve being the number of leaves left upon each plant after being topped.

Average height of plant when topped (Sept. 15) 39 inches.
Average length of largest leaves .. „ 23½ „
Average width of largest leaves .. „ 11¼ „

Estimated Balance Sheet.

Showing cost of production, and average value of a crop of one acre of Yellow Orinoco. The value of the produce of this variety being calculated upon the weight of 42 plants, as grown by Messrs. Carter, including all leaves, good, bad, and indifferent, which, when stripped from the stalks and cured, actually weighed 26 pounds, or equal to about 2,900 pounds per acre, allowing 4,840 plants per acre.

		£ s. d.
By Produce of Tobacco cured ready for sale to manufacturer, say 2,900 lbs. @ 4d.*		48 6 8
To Rent of Land and Buildings, including Rates, Tithes, and Taxes, @ 60/- per acre £3 0 0		
3 Ploughings @ 10/- per acre each time 1 10 0		
2 Harrowings @ 1/- per acre each time 0 2 0		
9 Loads Farm-yard Manure delivered on Land .. 2 8 0		
Spreading Farm-yard Manure 0 1 3		
3 cwt. Peruvian Guano @ £12 per ton 1 16 0		
5,000 Plants at about 15/- per 1,000 .. .. .. 3 15 0		
Planting ditto, 1 man 1 day 3/2, 1 boy 1 day 1/3 0 4 5		
2 Horse-hoeings @ 3/- per acre each time .. 0 6 0		
Manual labour, hilling and side-hoeing twice over @ 7/- per acre each time 0 14 0		
Pruning, topping, and suckering @ 8/- per acre .. 0 8 0		
Cutting @ 5/- per acre, carting to barn and hanging @ 12/- 0 17 0		
Firing, 2 loads waste hard wood to be found on the Farm (charge for labour only) 0 16 0		
Man's time curing and attending, etc., 2 weeks @ 15/- 1 10 0		
Stripping, sorting, bulking, and packing, say 2,900 lbs. @ 5/- per 100 lbs. 7 5 0		24 12 8
Average profit upon 1 acre		£23 14 0

* It is considered that 4d. per lb. is the lowest value at which average quality Tobacco can reasonably be placed.

TOBACCO—var. **GLASNER.**
Grown in Messrs. Carters' Field Crop, 1886.
Photographed on Wood.

TOBACCO—GLASNER.
(Semi-erect leaved.)

"HERE you have a splendid variety, with a fine cigar leaf," remarked a Virginian expert when inspecting Messrs. Carters' crop at Bromley. The "Glasner," however, is one of the latest to ripen, and therefore may be considered of less value to English growers than the earlier varieties.

Its fine habit and immense leaves are well represented in the opposite Illustration. The leaves are long and lance-shaped, the points, especially the lower ones, being blunted, with surface slightly corrugated as the plant develops; midrib, which is a pale green, is rather broad and somewhat woolly; the lesser ribs prominent, and of a bright greenish yellow colour—in substance thin and very gummy. Colour of flowers, rosy red.

The main stem is short, and remains covered by the upright growth of the upper leaves—there being an average distance of half an inch to an inch between the leaves, and thirteen to fifteen leaves upon a plant when topped.

Average height of plant when topped (Sept. 15) 30 inches.
Average length of largest leaves   ..   ,,   25½ ,,
Average width of largest leaves   ..   ,,   13½ ,,

Estimated Balance Sheet.

Showing cost of production, and average value of a crop of one acre of Glasner. The value of the produce of this variety being calculated upon the weight of 78 plants, as grown by Messrs. Carter, including all leaves, good, bad, and indifferent, which, when stripped from the stalks and cured, actually weighed 42 pounds, or equal to about 2,600 pounds per acre, allowing 4,840 plants per acre.

		£ s. d.	£ s. d.
By Produce of Tobacco cured ready for sale to manufacturer, say 2,600 lbs. @ 4d.*			43 6 8
To Rent of Land and Buildings, including Rates, Tithes, and Taxes, @ 60/- per acre	£3 0 0		
3 Ploughings @ 10/- per acre each time	1 10 0		
2 Harrowings @ 1/- per acre each time	0 2 0		
9 Loads Farm-yard Manure delivered on Land	2 8 0		
Spreading Farm-yard Manure	0 1 3		
3 cwt. Peruvian Guano @ £12 per ton	1 16 0		
5,000 Plants at about 15/- per 1,000	3 15 0		
Planting ditto, 1 man 1 day 3/2, 1 boy 1 day 1/3	0 4 5		
2 Horse-hoeings @ 3/- per acre each time	0 6 0		
Manual labour, hilling and side-hoeing twice over @ 7/- per acre each time	0 14 0		
Pruning, topping, and suckering @ 8/- per acre	0 8 0		
Cutting @ 5/- per acre, carting to barn and hanging @ 12/-	0 17 0		
Firing, 2 loads waste hard wood to be found on the Farm (charge for labour only)	0 16 0		
Man's time curing and attending, etc., 2 weeks @ 15/-	1 10 0		
Stripping, sorting, bulking, and packing, say 2,600 lbs. @ 5/- per 100 lbs.	6 10 0	23 17 8	
Average profit upon 1 acre			£19 9 0

* It is considered that 4d. per lb. *is the lowest value at which average quality Tobacco can reasonably be placed.*

TOBACCO—VAR. FLORIDA.
Grown in Messrs. Carters' Field Crop, 1886.
Photographed on Wood.

TOBACCO—FLORIDA.
(Horizontal leaved.)

This may be considered a *second early Tobacco* of average merit, although in most respects inferior to "Big Frederick."

As shown in the Illustration on the opposite page the leaves of "Florida" vary considerably in shape, inasmuch as whilst the lower ones are more or less blunted, the younger leaves are long and tapering. These become somewhat corrugated upon the surface as they ripen. The midrib is very broad, and of a pale green colour, the lesser ribs or veins being very faint and undefined. To the touch the leaves of this variety have a rough surface, fairly gummy, and are of a "leathery" texture. Colour of flowers, rich rose.

Very vigorous main stem showing an average distance of 2 inches between the leaves; nine to eleven leaves being the number left on each plant after being topped.

Average height of plant when topped (Sept. 15) 42 inches.
Average length of largest leaves .. ,, 27¼ ,,
Average width of largest leaves .. ,, 11¾ ,,

Estimated Balance Sheet.

Showing cost of production, and average value of a crop of one acre of Florida. The value of the produce of this variety being calculated upon the weight of 108 plants, as grown by Messrs. Carter, including all leaves, good, bad, and indifferent, which, when stripped from the stalks and cured, actually weighed 50 pounds, or equal to about 2,200 pounds per acre, allowing 4,840 plants per acre.

	£ s. d.	£ s. d.
By Produce of Tobacco cured ready for sale to manufacturer, say 2,200 lbs. @ 4d.*		36 13 4
To Rent of Land and Buildings, including Rates, Tithes, and Taxes. @ 60/- per acre	£3 0 0	
3 Ploughings @ 10/- per acre each time	1 10 0	
2 Harrowings @ 1/- per acre each time	0 2 0	
9 Loads Farm-yard Manure delivered on Land	2 8 0	
Spreading Farm-yard Manure	0 1 3	
3 cwt. Peruvian Guano @ £12 per ton	1 16 0	
5,000 Plants at about 15/- per 1,000	3 15 0	
Planting ditto, 1 man 1 day 3/2, 1 boy 1 day 1/3..	0 4 5	
2 Horse-hoeings @ 3/- per acre each time ..	0 6 0	
Manual labour, hilling and side-hoeing twice over @ 7/- per acre each time	0 14 0	
Pruning, topping, and suckering @ 8/- per acre ..	0 8 0	
Cutting @ 5/- per acre, carting to barn and hanging @ 12/-	0 17 0	
Firing, 2 loads waste hard wood to be found on the Farm (charge for labour only)	0 16 0	
Man's time curing and attending, etc., 2 weeks @ 15/-	1 10 0	
Stripping, sorting, bulking, and packing, say 2,200 lbs. @ 5/- per 100 lbs.	5 10 0	22 17 8
Average profit upon 1 acre		£13 15 8

* It is considered that 4d. per lb. *is the lowest value at which average quality Tobacco can reasonably be placed.*

TOBACCO—VAR. VIRGINIA.
Grown in Messrs. Carters' Field Crop, 1886.
Photographed on Wood.

TOBACCO—VIRGINIA.
(Horizontal leaved.)

It has been determined to class "Virginia" with the *first early Tobaccos*. In general character, and habit of growth, this variety resembles the "Big Frederick."

The Illustration on the opposite page affords a truthful picture of this plant.

The leaves are very long and tapering, and the surface of the matured leaf is more or less indented or corrugated. The midrib is of a greenish white colour, the lesser ribs or veins being prominent. Colour of flowers, bright rose.

As with "Big Frederick," the leaves are of considerable substance, and appear to contain less sap than the semi-erect varieties.

The main stem is hard and very strong—with an average distance of 2 to 2½ inches between the leaves—nine to eleven being the number of leaves left upon each plant after being topped.

Average height of plant when topped (Sept. 15)	37½	inches.
Average length of largest leaves	25	,,
Average width of largest leaves	11	,,

Estimated Balance Sheet.

Showing cost of production, and average value of a crop of one acre of Virginia. The value of the produce of this variety being calculated upon the weight of 72 plants, as grown by Messrs. Carter, including all leaves, good, bad, and indifferent, which, when stripped from the stalks and cured, actually weighed 37 pounds, or equal to about 2,420 pounds per acre, allowing 4,840 plants per acre.

	£ s. d.	
By Produce of Tobacco cured ready for sale to manufacturer, say 2,420 lbs. @ 4d.	40 6 8	
To Rent of Land and Buildings, including Rates, Tithes, and Taxes, @ 60/- per acre .. £3 0 0		
3 Ploughings @ 10/- per acre each time .. 1 10 0		
2 Harrowings @ 1/- per acre each time .. 0 2 0		
9 Loads Farm-yard Manure delivered on Land .. 2 8 0		
Spreading Farm-yard Manure .. 0 1 3		
3 cwt. Peruvian Guano @ £12 per ton .. 1 16 0		
5,000 Plants at about 15/- per 1,000 .. 3 15 0		
Planting ditto, 1 man 1 day 3/2, 1 boy 1 day 1/3 .. 0 4 5		
2 Horse-hoeings @ 3/- per acre each time.. 0 6 0		
Manual labour, hilling and side-hoeing twice over @ 7/- per acre each time.. 0 14 0		
Pruning, topping, and suckering @ 8/- per acre .. 0 8 0		
Cutting @ 5/- per acre, carting to barn and hanging @ 12/- 0 17 0		
Firing, 2 loads waste hard wood to be found on the Farm (charge for labour only).. 0 16 0		
Man's time curing and attending, etc., 2 weeks @ 15/- 1 10 0		
Stripping, sorting, bulking, and packing, say 2,420 lbs. @ 5/- per 100 lbs. .. 6 1 0	23 8 8	
Average profit upon 1 acre ..	£16 18 0	

* It is considered that 4d. per lb. *is the lowest value at which average quality Tobacco can reasonably be placed.*

TOBACCO—VAR. MARYLAND BROADLEAF.
Grown in Messrs. Carters' Field Crop, 1886.
Photographed on Wood.

TOBACCO—MARYLAND BROADLEAF.[39]
(Semi-erect leaved.)

This is probably one of the least desirable of the semi-erect class, as the plant matures slowly and the leaves do not dry so rapidly as many other sorts, after being housed.

It is, however, a handsome variety in growth, as shown by the opposite Illustration, and if planted out earlier it might make a better record in the future.

The leaves are long and tapering, of a rich sage-green colour, midrib rather broad, slightly woolly, and pale green, the lesser ribs or veins being prominent. As another consequence of late maturity the leaves of the broad leaf were less gummy than others. Colour of flowers, pale rose.

Stem short and stout, more or less hidden by the upper leaves, which are about 1 inch to 1½ inches apart, with nine to twelve leaves upon each plant after being topped.

Average height of plant when topped (Sept. 15) 38½ inches.
Average length of largest leaves .. „ 26 „
Average width of largest leaves .. „ 12½ „

Estimated Balance Sheet.

Showing cost of production, and average value of a crop of one acre of Maryland Broadleaf. The value of the produce of this variety being calculated upon the weight of 78 plants, as grown by Messrs. Carter, including all leaves, good, bad, and indifferent, which, when stripped from the stalks and cured, actually weighed 47 pounds, or equal to about 2,900 pounds per acre, allowing 4,840 plants per acre.

	£	s.	d.
By Produce of Tobacco cured ready for sale to manufacturer, say 2,900 lbs. @ 4d.*	48	6	8
To Rent of Land and Buildings, including Rates, Tithes, and Taxes, @ 60/- per acre ..£3 0 0			
3 Ploughings @ 10/- per acre each time .. 1 10 0			
2 Harrowings @ 1/- per acre each time .. 0 2 0			
9 Loads Farm-yard Manure delivered on Land .. 2 8 0			
Spreading Farm-yard Manure .. 0 1 3			
3 cwt. Peruvian Guano @ £12 per ton .. 1 16 0			
5,000 Plants at about 15/- per 1,000 .. 3 15 0			
Planting ditto, 1 man 1 day 3/2, 1 boy 1 day 1/3.. 0 4 5			
2 Horse-hoeings @ 3/- per acre each time.. 0 6 0			
Manual labour, hilling and side-hoeing twice over @ 7/- per acre each time.. 0 14 0			
Pruning, topping, and suckering @ 8/- per acre 0 8 0			
Cutting @ 5/- per acre, carting to barn and hanging @ 12/- 0 17 0			
Firing, 2 loads waste hard wood to be found on the Farm (charge for labour only).. 0 16 0			
Man's time curing and attending, etc., 2 weeks @ 15/- 1 10 0			
Stripping, sorting, bulking, and packing, say 2,900 lbs. @ 5/- per 100 lbs. .. 7 5 0	24	12	8
Average profit upon 1 acre	£23	14	0

* It is considered that 4d. per lb. *is the lowest value at which average quality Tobacco can reasonably be placed.*

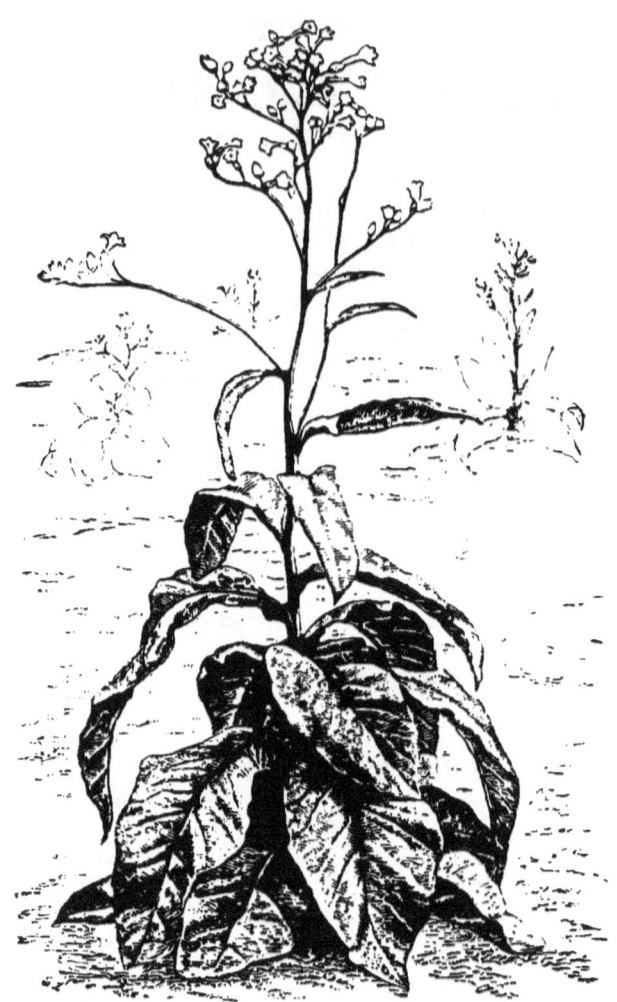

TOBACCO—VAR. CONNECTICUT.
Grown in Messrs. Carters' Field Crop, 1886.
Photographed on Wood.

TOBACCO—CONNECTICUT.
(Horizontal leaved.)

This variety—as shown in the Illustration on the opposite page—is quite distinct from the "Connecticut Seedleaf" figured at page 54, and is distinct in growth and general appearance. *It may be considered a second early variety.*

The leaves are long and less tapering at the point than some other varieties. The surface of the leaf becomes slightly corrugated as the plant matures; the midrib, which is of a pale yellowish green colour, is narrow, and the lesser ribs or veins are not prominent.

The leaves are very hard, gummy, and of considerable substance, having what may be termed a "leathery" character. Colour of flowers, pale rose.

The main stem is hard, and the plant appears to possess a vigorous constitution. An average distance of 2 inches between the leaves; ten to twelve leaves being the number left on each plant after being topped. It is generally admitted, however, that fourteen or fifteen leaves per plant might be grown of this variety with advantage.

Average height of plant when topped (Sept. 15) 45 inches.
Average length of largest leaves „ 31½ „
Average width of largest leaves „ 16½ „

Estimated Balance Sheet.

Showing cost of production, and average value of a crop of one acre of Connecticut. The value of the produce of this variety being calculated upon the weight of 18 plants, as grown by Messrs. Carter, including all leaves, good, bad, and indifferent, which, when stripped from the stalks and cured, actually weighed 10 pounds, or equal to about 2,600 pounds per acre, allowing 4,840 plants per acre.

	£ s. d.	£ s. d.
By Produce of Tobacco cured ready for sale to manufacturer; say 2,600 lbs. @ 4d.*		43 6 8
To Rent of Land and Buildings, including Rates, Tithes, and Taxes, @ 60/- per acre	£3 0 0	
3 Ploughings @ 10/- per acre each time	1 10 0	
2 Harrowings @ 1/- per acre each time	0 2 0	
9 Loads Farm-yard Manure delivered on Land	2 8 0	
Spreading Farm-yard Manure	0 1 3	
3 cwt. Peruvian Guano @ £12 per ton	1 16 0	
5,000 Plants at about 15/- per 1,000	3 15 0	
Planting ditto, 1 man 1 day 3/2, 1 boy 1 day 1/3	0 4 5	
2 Horse-hoeings @ 3/- per acre each time	0 6 0	
Manual labour, hilling and side-hoeing twice over @ 7/- per acre each time	0 14 0	
Pruning, topping, and suckering @ 8/- per acre	0 8 0	
Cutting @ 5/- per acre, carting to barn and hanging @ 12/-	0 17 0	
Firing, 2 loads waste hard wood to be found on the Farm (charge for labour only)	0 16 0	
Man's time curing and attending, etc., 2 weeks @ 15/-	1 10 0	
Stripping, sorting, bulking, and packing, say 2,600 lbs. @ 5/- per 100 lbs.	6 10 0	23 17 8
Average profit upon 1 acre		£19 9 0

* It is considered that 4d. per lb. *is the lowest value at which average quality Tobacco can reasonably be placed.*

TOBACCO—var. WHITE STEM.
Grown in Messrs. Carters' Field Crop, 1886.
Photographed on Wood.

TOBACCO—WHITE STEM.
(Horizontal leaved.)

This may be considered a *second early* variety of considerable merit, and very distinct in general characteristics. Its unique appearance is faithfully reproduced in the Illustration upon the opposite page.

The leaves are of medium length, less tapering in form than some other kinds—slightly corrugated—of great substance, becoming very gummy as they mature.

A marked peculiarity possessed by this variety is the *white midrib of the leaf or stem*, as it is designated in America—the lesser ribs or veins being of a pale green colour and clearly defined. Colour of flowers, very faint rose.

The main stem is somewhat slender, but very hard in texture, with an average distance of $1\frac{1}{2}$ to 2 inches between the leaves, nine to eleven leaves being the number left upon each plant after being topped.

Average height of plant when topped (Sept. 15) 38 inches.
Average length of largest leaves .. ,, 25 ,,
Average width of largest leaves .. ,, 11 ,,

Estimated Balance Sheet.

Showing cost of production, and average value of a crop of one acre of White Stem. The value of the produce of this variety being calculated upon the weight of 72 plants, as grown by Messrs. Carter, including all leaves, good, bad, and indifferent, which, when stripped from the stalks and cured, actually weighed 36 pounds, or equal to about 2,420 pounds per acre, allowing 4,840 plants per acre.

		£	s.	d.
By Produce of Tobacco cured ready for sale to manufacturer, say 2,420 lbs. @ 4d.*		40	6	8
To Rent of Land and Buildings, including Rates, Tithes, and Taxes, @ 60/- per acre £3 0 0				
3 Ploughings @ 10/- per acre each time 1 10 0				
2 Harrowings @ 1/- per acre each time 0 2 0				
9 Loads Farm-yard Manure delivered on Land 2 8 0				
Spreading Farm-yard Manure 0 1 3				
3 cwt. Peruvian Guano @ £12 per ton 1 16 0				
5,000 Plants at about 15/- per 1,000 3 15 0				
Planting ditto, 1 man 1 day 3/2, 1 boy 1 day 1/3 0 4 5				
2 Horse-hoeings @ 3/- per acre each time 0 6 0				
Manual labour, hilling and side-hoeing twice over @ 7/- per acre each time 0 14 0				
Pruning, topping, and suckering @ 8/- per acre 0 8 0				
Cutting @ 5/- per acre, carting to barn and hanging @ 12/- 0 17 0				
Firing, 2 loads waste hard wood to be found on the Farm (charge for labour only) 0 16 0				
Man's time curing and attending, etc., 2 weeks @ 15/- 1 10 0				
Stripping, sorting, bulking, and packing, say 2,420 lbs. @ 5/- per 100 lbs. 6 1 0		23	8	8
Average profit upon 1 acre		£16	18	0

* It is considered that 4d. per lb. *is the lowest value at which average quality Tobacco can reasonably be placed.*

TOBACCO—VAR. PENNSYLVANIA.

Grown in Messrs. Carters' Field Crop, 1886.
Photographed on Wood.

TOBACCO—PENNSYLVANIA.
(Semi-erect leaved.)

THIS is *a late variety*, ripening off very slowly in the Tobacco house. As an instance of this it was observed that on October 23rd, or fully a month after being housed, the leaves of "Pennsylvania" remained more or less green in colour, whereas those of nearly all other varieties presented varied hues of yellow and brown.

As evidenced by the Illustration opposite, it forms a handsome specimen in the crop, the large and long pointed leaves being of a rich pea-green shade with woolly midrib and lesser ribs or veins of a pale yellow colour, the latter less prominent than with the "Maryland" (see page 38). Leaves gummy and of fair substance. Colour of flowers, very pale pink.

The stem, which is of a creamy yellow colour, stout and short, is hidden by the foliage, leaves about an inch apart, and eleven to thirteen upon each "topped" plant.

Average height of plant when topped (Sept. 15)	32½	inches.
Average length of largest leaves .. „	23	„
Average width of largest leaves .. „	9½	„

Estimated Balance Sheet.

Showing cost of production, and average value of a crop of one acre of Pennsylvania. The value of the produce of this variety being calculated upon the weight of 102 plants, as grown by Messrs. Carter, including all leaves, good, bad, and indifferent, which, when stripped from the stalks and cured, actually weighed 48 pounds, or equal to about 2,400 pounds per acre, allowing 4,840 plants per acre.

	£	s.	d.			
By Produce of Tobacco cured ready for sale to manufacturer, say 2,400 lbs. @ 4d.*				40	0	0
To Rent of Land and Buildings, including Rates, Tithes, and Taxes, @ 60/- per acre £3 0 0						
3 Ploughings @ 10/- per acre each time 1 10 0						
2 Harrowings @ 1/- per acre each time 0 2 0						
9 Loads Farm-yard Manure delivered on Land 2 8 0						
Spreading Farm-yard Manure 0 1 3						
3 cwt. Peruvian Guano @ £12 per ton 1 16 0						
5,000 Plants at about 15 - per 1,000 .. .. .. 3 15 0						
Planting ditto, 1 man 1 day 3/2, 1 boy 1 day 1/3 .. .. 0 4 5						
2 Horse-hoeings @ 3/- per acre each time 0 6 0						
Manual labour, hilling and side-hoeing twice over @ 7/- per acre each time 0 14 0						
Pruning, topping, and suckering @ 8/- per acre .. 0 8 0						
Cutting @ 5/- per acre, carting to barn and hanging @ 12/- 0 17 0						
Firing, 2 loads waste hard wood to be found on the Farm (charge for labour only) 0 16 0						
Man's time, curing and attending, etc., 2 weeks @ 15/- 1 10 0						
Stripping, sorting, bulking, and packing, say 2,400 lbs. @ 5/- per 100 lbs. 6 0 0				23	7	8
Average profit upon 1 acre				£16	12	4

* It is considered that 4d. per lb. *is the lowest value at which average quality Tobacco can reasonably be placed.*

TOBACCO—VAR. HESTER VIRGINIA.
Grown in MESSRS. CARTERS' FIELD CROP, 1886.
Photographed on Wood.

TOBACCO—HESTER VIRGINIA.
(Horizontal leaved.)

This variety should rank as a *first early* Tobacco, and is in many other respects to be commended. It is also stated to be the most promising of all the varieties grown by Mr. Bateman, of Brightlingsea, from seeds obtained from Messrs. Carter.

The leaves are of medium length, broad or club-formed —as shown in the Illustration upon the opposite page— becoming somewhat corrugated as the plant matures. The midrib, which is slightly woolly, is of a greenish white colour, the lesser ribs or veins being very prominent and of a pale green shade. The leaves are of a stout leathery texture, of considerable substance and very gummy. Colour of flowers, pale rose.

The main stem is less hard than some other kinds, and is also of a peculiar shade of green. The plant is vigorous— an average distance of 2 inches between the leaves—nine to eleven leaves being the number left upon each plant after being topped.

Average height of plant when topped (Sept. 15) 40 inches.
Average length of largest leaves .. ,, 24½ ,,
Average width of largest leaves .. ,, 13¼ ,,

Estimated Balance Sheet.

Showing cost of production, and average value of a crop of one acre of Hester Virginia. The value of the produce of this variety being calculated upon the weight of 5½ plants, as grown by Messrs. Carter, including all leaves, good, bad, and indifferent, which, when stripped from the stalks and cured, actually weighed 33 pounds, or equal to about 2,900 pounds per acre, allowing 4,840 plants per acre.

	£	s.	d.
By Produce of Tobacco cured ready for sale to manufacturer, say 2,900 lbs. @ 4d.*	48	6	8

	£	s.	d.			
To Rent of Land and Buildings, including Rates, Tithes, and Taxes, @ 60/- per acre	3	0	0			
3 Ploughings @ 10/- per acre each time	1	10	0			
2 Harrowings @ 1/- per acre each time	0	2	0			
9 Loads Farm-yard Manure delivered on Land ..	2	8	0			
Spreading Farm-yard Manure	0	1	3			
3 cwt. Peruvian Guano @ £12 per ton	1	16	0			
5,000 Plants at about 15/- per 1,000	3	15	0			
Planting ditto, 1 man 1 day 3 2, 1 boy 1 day 1/3 ..	0	4	5			
2 Horse-hoeings @ 3/- per acre each time ..	0	6	0			
Manual labour, hilling and side-hoeing twice over @ 7/- per acre each time	0	14	0			
Pruning, topping, and suckering @ 8/- per acre ..	0	8	0			
Cutting @ 5/- per acre, carting to barn and hanging @ 12/-	0	17	0			
Firing, 2 loads waste hard wood to be found on the Farm (charge for labour only)	0	16	0			
Man's time curing and attending, etc., 2 weeks @ 15/-	1	10	0			
Stripping, sorting, bulking, and packing, say 2,900 lbs. @ 5/- per 100 lbs.	7	5	0	24	12	8
Average profit upon 1 acre				£23	14	0

* It is considered that 4d. per lb. *is the lowest value at which average quality Tobacco can reasonably be placed.*

TOBACCO—VAR. ISLAND BROADLEAF.

Grown in Messrs. Carters' Field Crop, 1886.
Photographed on Wood.

TOBACCO—ISLAND BROADLEAF.
(Semi-erect leaved.)

This is a distinct and showy variety in growth, the entire plant being of a peculiarly pretty sage-green colour.

As shown in the Illustration, the leaves are large, broad, and tapering, the tips of the lower ones being rather blunt, the surface of the leaf, which handles "thin" as compared with some others, is even and regular, and remarkably gummy as the plant matures.

The midrib is of a pale yellowish green colour, rather broad and woolly, the lesser ribs or veins being very pronounced. Colour of flowers, bright rose.

The main stem—like the "Glasner"—is short when topped, and remains hidden by the upright growth of the upper leaves; average distance of about an inch between the leaves, with thirteen to fifteen leaves upon a plant.

Average height of plant when topped (Sept. 15) 38 inches.
Average length of largest leaves .. ,, 29 ,,
Average width of largest leaves .. ,, 14 ,,

Estimated Balance Sheet.

Showing cost of production, and average value of a crop of one acre of Island Broadleaf. The value of the produce of this variety being calculated upon the estimated weight of 72 plants, as grown by Messrs. Carter, including all leaves, good, bad, and indifferent, which, when stripped from the stalks and cured, were judged to weigh 48 pounds (but this variety was not actually weighed), or equal to about 3,200 pounds per acre, allowing 4,840 plants per acre. The absence of actual weights in this particular instance is accounted for from the fact that Messrs. Carter had begun to pack down the variety before they thought of putting the Tobacco upon the scales.

	£	s.	d.
By Produce of Tobacco cured ready for sale to manufacturer, say 3,200 lbs. @ 4d. ..	53	6	8
To Rent of Land and Buildings, including Rates, Tithes, and Taxes, @ 60/- per acre £3 0 0			
3 Ploughings @ 10/- per acre each time 1 10 0			
2 Harrowings @ 1/- per acre each time 0 2 0			
9 Loads Farm-yard Manure delivered on Land .. 2 8 0			
Spreading Farm-yard Manure 0 1 3			
3 cwt. Peruvian Guano @ £12 per ton 1 16 0			
5,000 Plants at about 15/- per 1,000 .. 3 15 0			
Planting ditto, 1 man 1 day 3/2, 1 boy 1 day 1/3 0 4 5			
2 Horse-hoeings @ 3/- per acre each time 0 6 0			
Manual labour, hilling and side-hoeing twice over @ 7/- per acre each time.. 0 14 0			
Pruning, topping, and suckering @ 8/- per acre 0 8 0			
Cutting @ 5/- per acre, carting to barn and hanging @ 12/- 0 17 0			
Firing, 2 loads waste hard wood to be found on the Farm (charge for labour only) .. 0 16 0			
Man's time curing and attending, etc., 2 weeks @ 15/- 1 10 0			
Stripping, sorting, bulking, and packing, say 3,200 lbs. @ 5/- per 100 lbs. .. 8 0 0	25	7	8
Average profit upon 1 acre ..	£27	19	0

* It is considered that 4d. per lb. *is the lowest value at which average quality Tobacco can reasonably be placed.*

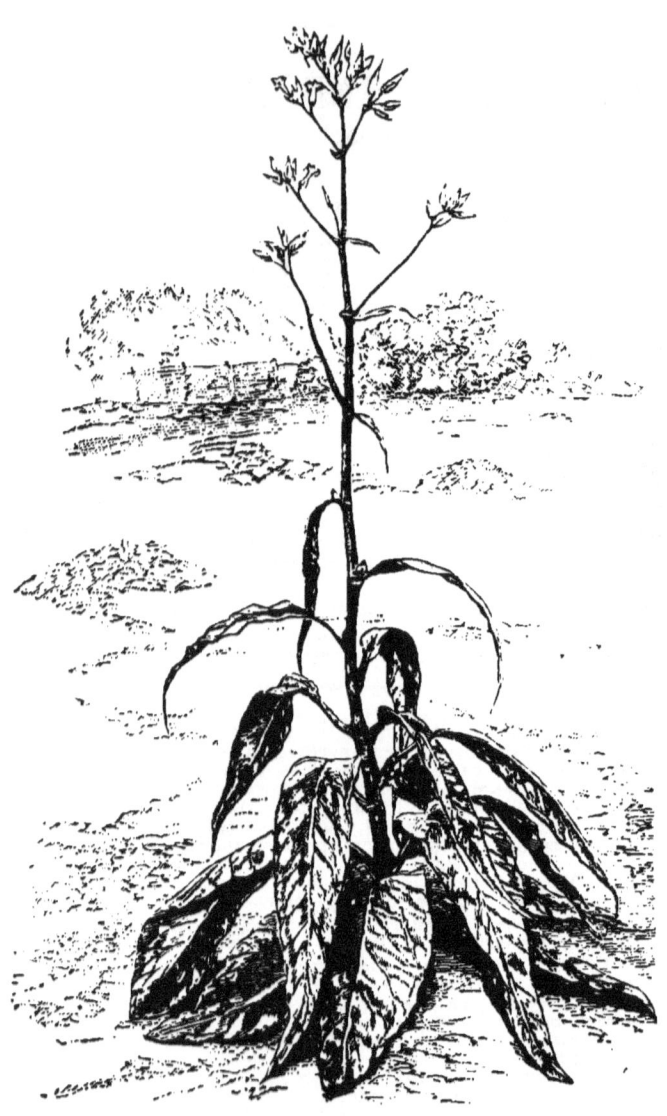

TOBACCO—VAR. ONE SUCKER.

Grown in MESSRS. CARTERS' FIELD CROP, 1886.
Photographed on Wood.

TOBACCO—ONE SUCKER.
(Horizontal leaved.)

This variety—as evinced by the Illustration upon the opposite page—possesses a distinct individuality, and appears well adapted to our English climate, the crop being estimated as one of the very heaviest.

The leaves are long, tapering, and narrow—the surface but little indented.

The midrib is of a pale greenish white and the lesser ribs or veins are very clearly defined. Colour of flowers, deep rose.

The main stem is stout and very hard, showing an average distance of 1½ to 2 inches between the leaves—eleven to twelve leaves being the number left upon each plant after being topped.

Average height of plant when topped (Sept. 15) 36 inches.
Average length of largest leaves .. ,, 26½ ,,
Average width of largest leaves .. ,, 8¼ ,,

Estimated Balance Sheet.

Showing cost of production, and average value of a crop of one acre of One Sucker. The value of the produce of this variety being calculated upon the estimated weight of 78 plants, as grown by Messrs. Carter, including all leaves, good, bad, and indifferent, which, when stripped from the stalks and cured, were judged to weigh 50 pounds (but this variety was not actually weighed), or equal to about 3,000 pounds per acre, allowing 4,840 plants per acre.

The absence of actual weights in this particular instance is accounted for from the fact that Messrs. Carter had begun to pack down the variety before they thought of putting the Tobacco upon the scales.

	£ s. d.	£ s. d.
By Produce of Tobacco cured ready for sale to manufacturer, say 3,000 lbs. @ 4d.* ..		50 0 0
To Rent of Land and Buildings, including Rates, Tithes, and Taxes, @ 60/- per acre ..	£3 0 0	
3 Ploughings @ 10/- per acre each time ..	1 10 0	
2 Harrowings @ 1/- per acre each time ..	0 2 0	
9 Loads Farm-yard Manure delivered on Land ..	2 8 0	
Spreading Farm-yard Manure ..	0 1 3	
3 cwt. Peruvian Guano @ £12 per ton ..	1 16 0	
5,000 Plants at about 15/- per 1,000 ..	3 15 0	
Planting ditto, 1 man 1 day 3/2, 1 boy 1 day 1/3 ..	0 4 5	
2 Horse-hoeings @ 3/- per acre each time ..	0 6 0	
Manual labour, hilling and side-hoeing twice over @ 7/- per acre each time ..	0 14 0	
Pruning, topping, and suckering @ 8/- per acre ..	0 8 0	
Cutting @ 5/- per acre, carting to barn and hanging @ 12/-	0 17 0	
Firing, 2 loads waste hard wood to be found on the Farm (charge for labour only) ..	0 16 0	
Man's time curing and attending, etc., 2 weeks @ 15/-	1 10 0	
Stripping, sorting, bulking, and packing, say 3,000 lbs. @ 5/- per 100 lbs. ..	7 10 0	24 17 8
Average profit upon 1 acre ..		£25 2 4

* It is considered that 4d. per lb. *is the lowest value at which average quality Tobacco can reasonably be placed.*

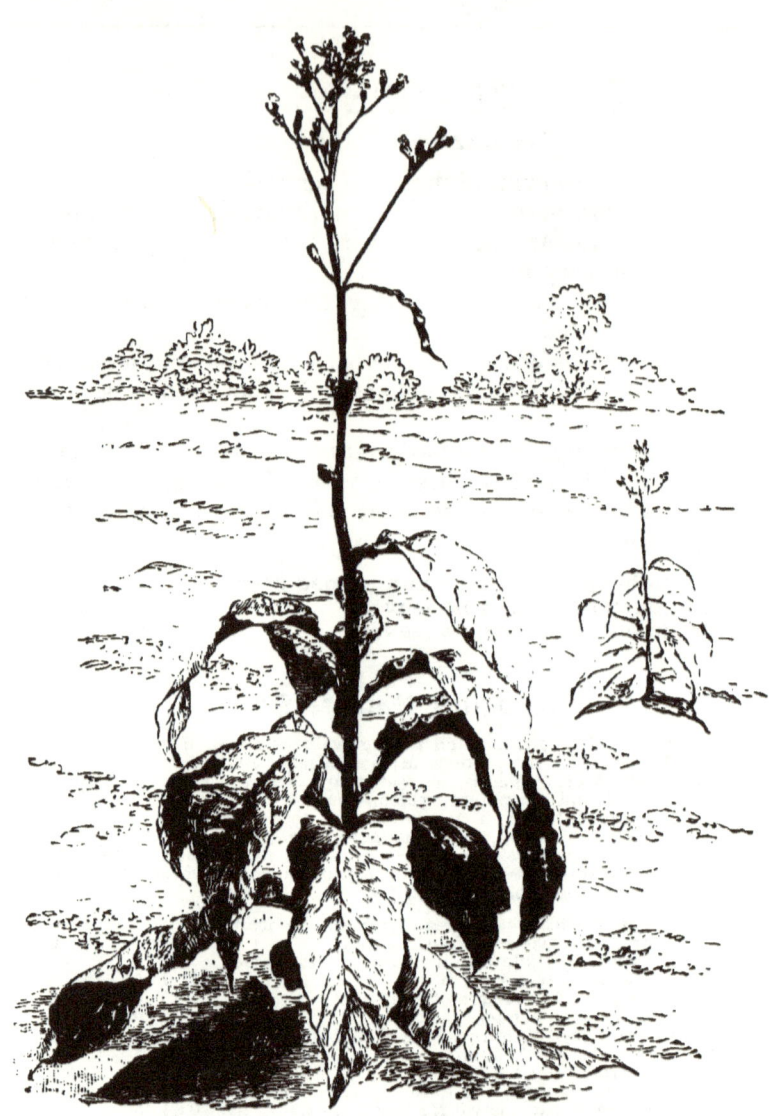

TOBACCO—var. BIG FREDERICK.
Grown in Messrs. Carters' Field Crop, 1886.
Photographed on Wood.

TOBACCO—BIG FREDERICK.
(Horizontal leaved.)

This is very distinct as well as being *one of the earliest* and most productive of all the horizontal or drooping-foliaged varieties. It is a strong grower, and appeared to thrive equally with any other kind in our English climate.

The leaves—as shown in the Illustration on the opposite page—are very long, somewhat lance-shaped, with points of medium length.

As the plants mature the surface of the leaf of this variety becomes considerably corrugated, the outer edges showing indications of a faint yellow colouring as they ripen upon the plant. The midrib is of a pale yellowish green colour, the lesser ribs or veins being very acute and marked. Colour of flowers, rosy salmon.

The leaves of "Big Frederick" are of immense substance, and, although very gummy, appear to be less sappy than many varieties of the semi-erect types. The main stem is hard and thick, with an average distance of about 2 inches between the leaves; nine leaves being left on each plant after being "topped."

Average height of plant when topped (Sept. 15)   40 inches.
Average length of largest leaves   ..   „   27   „
Average width of largest leaves   ..   „   13¾ „

Estimated Balance Sheet.

Showing cost of production, and average value of a crop of one acre of Big Frederick. The value of the produce of this variety being calculated upon the estimated weight of 72 plants, as grown by Messrs. Carter, including all leaves, good, bad, and indifferent, which, when stripped from the stalks and cured, were judged to weigh 45 pounds (but this variety was not actually weighed), or equal to about 3,000 pounds per acre, allowing 4,840 plants per acre.

The absence of actual weights in this particular instance is accounted for from the fact that Messrs. Carter had begun to pack down the variety before they thought of putting the Tobacco upon the scales.

	£ s. d.	
By Produce of Tobacco cured ready for sale to manufacturer, say 3,000 lbs. @ 4d.* ..	50 0 0	
To Rent of Land and Buildings, including Rates, Tithes, and Taxes, @ 60/- per acre £3 0 0		
3 Ploughings @ 10/- per acre each time 1 10 0		
2 Harrowings @ 1/- per acre each time 0 2 0		
9 Loads Farm-yard Manure delivered on Land 2 8 0		
Spreading Farm-yard Manure 0 1 3		
3 cwt. Peruvian Guano @ £12 per ton 1 16 0		
5,000 Plants at about 15/- per 1,000 .. .. .. 3 15 0		
Planting ditto, 1 man 1 day 3/2, 1 boy 1 day 1/3.. .. 0 4 5		
2 Horse-hoeings @ 3/- per acre each time.. .. .. 0 6 0		
Manual labour, hilling and side-hoeing twice over @ 7/- per acre each time.. .. .. 0 14 0		
Pruning, topping, and suckering @ 8/- per acre .. 0 8 0		
Cutting @ 5/- per acre, carting to barn and hanging @ 12/- 0 17 0		
Firing, 2 loads waste hard wood to be found on the Farm (charge for labour only).. .. .. .. 0 16 0		
Man's time curing and attending, etc., 2 weeks @ 15/- 1 10 0		
Stripping, sorting, bulking, and packing, say 3,000 lbs. @ 5/- per 100 lbs. 7 10 0	24 17 8	
Average profit upon 1 acre	£25 2 4	

* It is considered that 4d. per lb. *is the lowest value at which average quality Tobacco can reasonably be placed.*

TOBACCO—VAR. CONNECTICUT SEEDLEAF.
Grown in Messrs. Carters' Field Crop, 1886.
Photographed on Wood.

TOBACCO—CONNECTICUT SEEDLEAF.
(Semi-erect leaved.)

This variety is distinct from the "Connecticut" described at page 41. It may be considered a *second early variety* of very considerable merit.

It is undoubtedly one of the best of the semi-erect habited section, its magnificent foliage—as represented in the Illustration opposite—rendering it at once remarkable when seen for the first time in growth. The lower leaves are somewhat full at the point, the upper ones being more pointed. The surface of the leaf continues even as the plants mature, but becomes very gummy. The midrib is of a pale lemon yellow colour, the lesser ribs or veins being prominent. In growth the substance of the leaf appears to be thinner or more of the consistency of paper than the section represented by "Big Frederick." Colour of flowers, rosy salmon.

The main stem when topped, is also much shorter, with an average distance of about 1½ inches between the leaves, with ten to twelve leaves upon each plant.

Average height of plant when topped (Sept. 15) 39½ inches.
Average length of largest leaves   „   29½   „
Average width of largest leaves   „   13¼   „

Estimated Balance Sheet.

Showing cost of production, and average value of a crop of one acre of Connecticut Seedleaf. The value of the produce of this variety being calculated upon the estimated weight of 90 plants, as grown by Messrs. Carter, including all leaves, good, bad, and indifferent, which, when stripped from the stalks and cured, were judged to weigh 50 pounds (but this variety was not actually weighed), or equal to about 2,600 pounds per acre, allowing 4,840 plants per acre. The absence of actual weights in this particular instance is accounted for from the fact that Messrs. Carter had begun to pack down the variety before they thought of putting the Tobacco upon the scales.

	£ s. d.	£ s. d.
By Produce of Tobacco cured ready for sale to manufacturer, say 2,600 lbs. @ 4d.		43 6 8
To Rent of Land and Buildings, including Rates, Tithes, and Taxes, @ 60/- per acre	3 0 0	
3 Ploughings @ 10/- per acre each time	1 10 0	
2 Harrowings @ 1/- per acre each time	0 2 0	
9 Loads Farm-yard Manure delivered on Land	2 8 0	
Spreading Farm-yard Manure	0 1 3	
3 cwt. Peruvian Guano @ £12 per ton	1 16 0	
5,000 Plants at about 15/- per 1,000	3 15 0	
Planting ditto, 1 man 1 day 3/2, 1 boy 1 day 1/3	0 4 5	
2 Horse-hoeings @ 3/- per acre each time	0 6 0	
Manual labour, hilling and side-hoeing twice over @ 7/- per acre each time	0 14 0	
Pruning, topping, and suckering @ 8/- per acre	0 8 0	
Cutting @ 5/- per acre, carting to barn and hanging @ 12/-	0 17 0	
Firing, 2 loads waste hard wood to be found on the Farm (charge for labour only)	0 16 0	
Man's time curing and attending, etc., 2 weeks @ 15/-	1 10 0	
Stripping, sorting, bulking, and packing, say 2,600 lbs. @ 5/- per 100 lbs.	6 10 0	23 17 8
Average profit upon 1 acre		£19 9 0

* It is considered that 4d. per lb. *is the lowest value at which average quality Tobacco can reasonably be placed.*

TOBACCO–VAR. HAVANA.

In consequence of the specimen plant reserved for Illustration being wilfully destroyed, we failed to get a photograph of this variety.

TOBACCO—HAVANA.
(Horizontal leaved.)

A distinct and *first early variety* of less vigorous growth and habit than most others; for this reason a greater number of leaves might be left upon each plant with advantage.

It may be described as of somewhat short or stunted growth, leaves long and tapering, slightly corrugated, and of a leathery substance. The midrib is of a yellowish white colour, and slightly woolly, the lesser ribs or veins being very delicate. Colour of flowers undetermined, for reasons stated opposite.

Main stem slender but very strong in texture, leaves drooping, with an average distance of 1½ inches from each other, eleven to twelve leaves being the number left upon each plant after being topped.

Average height of plant when topped (Sept. 15) 37½ inches.
Average length of largest leaves .. ,, 20 ,,
Average width of largest leaves .. ,, 10½ ,,

Estimated Balance Sheet.

Showing cost of production, and average value of a crop of one acre of Havana. The value of the produce of this variety being calculated upon the estimated weight of 12 plants, as grown by Messrs. Carter, including all leaves, good, bad, and indifferent, which, when stripped from the stalks and cured, were judged to weigh 3 pounds (but this variety was not actually weighed), or equal to about 1,210 pounds per acre, allowing 4,840 plants per acre.

The absence of actual weights in this particular instance is accounted for from the fact that Messrs. Carter had begun to pack down the variety before they thought of putting the Tobacco upon the scales.

		£ s. d.	
By Produce of Tobacco cured ready for sale to manufacturer, say 1,210 lbs. @ 4d.		20 3 4	
To Rent of Land and Buildings, including Rates, Tithes, and Taxes, @ 60/- per acre	£3 0 0		
3 Ploughings @ 10/- per acre each time	1 10 0		
2 Harrowings @ 1/- per acre each time	0 2 0		
9 Loads Farm-yard Manure delivered on Land	2 8 0		
Spreading Farm-yard Manure	0 1 3		
3 cwt. Peruvian Guano @ £12 per ton	1 16 0		
5,000 Plants at about 15/- per 1,000	3 15 0		
Planting ditto, 1 man 1 day 3/2, 1 boy 1 day 1/3	0 4 5		
2 Horse-hoeings @ 3/- per acre each time	0 6 0		
Manual labour, hilling and side-hoeing twice over @ 7/- per acre each time	0 14 0		
Pruning, topping, and suckering @ 8/- per acre	0 8 0		
Cutting @ 5/- per acre, carting to barn and hanging @ 12/-	0 17 0		
Firing, 2 loads waste hard wood to be found on the Farm (charge for labour only)	0 16 0		
Man's time curing and attending, etc., 2 weeks @ 15/-	1 10 0		
Stripping, sorting, bulking, and packing, say 1,210 lbs. @ 5/- per 100 lbs.	3 0 6	20 8	
Average loss upon 1 acre		£0 4 10	

* It is considered that 4d. per lb. *is the lowest value at which average quality Tobacco can reasonably be placed.*

DESCRIPTION OF THE CULTIVATION

OF

MESSRS. CARTERS' TOBACCO CROP.

Messrs. Carters' Tobacco crop comprised an area of about three-quarters of an acre, the land—which was hired at a high rental, but conveniently near to London, and permitting of a daily inspection, whereas Messrs. Carters' Seed Farms are some seventy miles distant—being almost a dead flat, low-lying, and so indifferently drained, that in May last, and less than a month from the period at which the land was planted, some parts were almost under water. From this cause also it was found impossible to obtain the fine tilth considered as most desirable in the production of Tobacco. The land partook more or less of three characters, the lower portion

DESCRIPTION OF THE CULTIVATION. 59

being a black vegetable deposit, retaining the moisture most tenaciously, the middle section was a rich sandy loam, whilst the top end of the field worked off to a light gravelly soil.

The Tobacco Seeds were sown on hotbeds, April 7th, 1886 (very late), and the slow growth made by the plants in the earliest stages was most disappointing; this, however, was partly accounted for by the prevalence of unusually cold east winds, to the effects of which the plants were more or less subject, inasmuch as if the hotbeds had been kept close, the plants would have become "drawn," "weakly," and unsuitable.

As a consequence it was found quite impossible to plant the land as early as had been contemplated, and it was not effected until June 16th, when, the land having been ploughed into ridges three feet apart, the Tobacco plants were put into the ground at a uniform distance of three feet from each other, and thoroughly well watered. The weather then appeared more promising, but almost immediately afterwards the wind again veered round to the north-east, and a week of dreadfully cold and sunless weather was experienced.

These very ungenial atmospheric conditions were succeeded by nearly a month of persistent sunshine by day, whilst the night temperature registered unpleasantly low, with an utter absence of rain until July 7th, when a few drops fell for the first time upon the plants. From this period the following particulars mark the development of the crop, at the same time showing the anxious solicitude evinced by the Board of Inland Revenue :

July 8.—*Excise officer made first visit.*
,, 17.—Stormy. Plants growing very fast.
,, 19.—Tobacco hoed the second time.
,, 20.—Heavy rains.
,, 23.—Stormy. Tobacco growing rapidly.
,, 27.—Commenced "earthing up" Tobacco.
,, 29.—*Excise officer made second visit.*
Aug. 5.—Finished "earthing up" Tobacco.
,, 9.—Commenced "topping" the Tobacco.
,, 11.—*Excise officer made third visit.*
,, 12.—Tobacco hoed the fourth time.
,, 20.—*Excise officer made fourth visit.*
,, 24.—"Suckering" the Tobacco.
,, 26.—Found first caterpillars attacking plants.
,, 28.—Closed an extremely hot week.
Sept. 7.—*Excise officer made fifth visit.*
,, 10.—Tobacco beginning to ripen.
,, 11.—Slight frost at night.
,, 13.—*Excise officer made sixth visit.*
,, 17.—Sharp frost, dry east wind.
,, 18.—Another frost. Commenced cutting Tobacco.
,, 27.—Finished cutting and housing Tobacco.

The following record made by Messrs. Carter shows the average weekly height of each variety (at the later periods after being topped), *i.e.*, after removing the head or flowering stem:

Variety.	June 23.	June 30.	July 7.	July 14.	July 21.	July 28.	Aug. 4.	Aug. 11.	Aug. 18.	Aug. 25.	Sept. 1.	Sept. 8.	Sept. 15.	Average length of largest leaves.	Average width of largest leaves.
	in.	in.	in.	in.	in.	in.	in.	in.	in.	in.	in.	in.	in.	in.	in.
Big Frederick	3	4	6	9	12	18	27	36	39	41½	42½	44½	41½	27	13¾
Conn. Seed Leaf	3	3	4	7	9	12	16	24	29	33	37	39	39½	29½	13¾
Connecticut ..	3	4	5	8	12	15	21	29	34	39	42½	43½	45	31½	16½
Florida	3	4	6	7	12	16	23	30	34	38	40	41½	42	27¾	11¾
Glasner	3	3	4	5	7	9	13	18	21	23	27	29	30	25½	13½
Havana	3	4	5	7	10	12	16	22	26	31	36	37	37½	20	10½
Hester Virginia	3	4	5	9	12	16	21	28	34	36	38	39	40	24½	13¾
Island B. Leaf	3	3	4	7	10	14	20	26	29	32½	36	37	38	29	14
Kentucky ..	3	3	4	6	8	11	16	22	25	27½	30½	32½	33	27½	13
Maryland B. Lf.	3	4	5	8	12	15	22	29	34	36	37	38	38½	26	12½
One Sucker ..	3	3	4	6	9	12	19	25	28	31	33½	34½	36	26½	6¾
Pennsylvania, 1	3	3	5	7	8	10	14	20	23	26	30	31½	32½	23	9½
Pennsylvania, 2	3	3	5	6	8	11	16	21	24	28	32½	33	34	26	12
Virginia ..	3	4	6	9	12	16	23	29	33	35½	36½	37	37½	25	11
White Burleigh	3	3	4	6	9	12	17	22	24	27	30	32	34	27	12½
White Stem ..	3	3	4	6	10	13	16	22	27	32	36	37½	38	25	11
Yellow Orinoco	3	4	5	6	8	10	15	21	27	32	37	38½	39	23½	11¼
Yellow Prior ..	3	4	5	7	11	14	22	30	36	42	44	45	46	27	14¾

AVERAGE WEEKLY HEIGHT WHEN TOPPED.

It will be observed from the above statistics, that the principal growth was made during the month of August, but in an ordinary spring the planting of the crop may be safely conducted about the middle of May, when the harvest would be proportionately early—a most desirable consummation, as rendering the after curing more simple and certain.

The following Table shows the average relative weight of each variety, and in addition the aggregate production of the entire crop, which comprised 3,846 plants at the time of cutting:

WEIGHT OF GREEN CROP WHEN HOUSED, INCLUDING CENTRE STALK, THE PLANTS HAVING LAID ABOUT 24 HOURS UPON THE GROUND TO WITHER BEFORE HOUSING.

	Number of Plants.	Total Weight in lbs.	Average Weight per Plant.
		lbs.	lbs.
Big Frederick	262	$317\frac{1}{2}$	$1\frac{1}{4}$
Conn. Seedleaf	269	$464\frac{1}{2}$	$1\frac{3}{4}$
Connecticut	54	82	$1\frac{1}{2}$
Florida	316	$385\frac{1}{2}$	$1\frac{1}{4}$
Glasner	252	430	$1\frac{3}{4}$
Havana	56	44	$\frac{3}{4}$
Hester Virginia	242	256	1
Island Broadleaf	258	498	2
Kentucky	253	338	$1\frac{1}{4}$
Maryland Broadleaf	319	406	$1\frac{1}{4}$
One Sucker	250	355	$1\frac{1}{6}$
Pennsylvania	320	486	$1\frac{1}{2}$
White Burleigh	242	278	$1\frac{1}{4}$
Virginia	247	243	1
White Stem	254	292	1
Yellow Orinoco	191	207	1
Yellow Prior	61	79	$1\frac{1}{4}$
	3,846	$5,161\frac{1}{2}$	

The plants being placed a yard apart every way, and the number of plants thus occupying an acre being 4,840, the total weight produced per acre (upon the above average) would be about 6,200 lbs.

Experts calculate that the plants shrink at least 60 to 75 per cent. in the process of drying and stripping from the main stem, so that there should remain about 12 to 24 cwt. of tobacco from an acre, available for disposal to the manufacturer at a price ranging from fourpence per pound according to the quality.

It will be admitted that these figures point to the cultivation of Tobacco as a remunerative occupation, and it may reasonably be expected that if at any future time the Government in their wisdom can devise means to collect the revenue in a way which shall not unduly interfere with the interests of the home producer, and without endangering the sum total of this important source of revenue, the cultivation of Tobacco as a staple crop will soon become universal in those districts best adapted to its requirements.

HARVESTING MESSRS. CARTERS' TOBACCO CROP.

The process of harvesting was as follows: A certain number of men were provided with ordi-

"PICKING UP" MESSRS. CARTERS' GREEN CROP OF TOBACCO.

nary shoemakers' knives, and proceeded to cut the plants row by row, severing them just above

HARVESTING THE TOBACCO CROP.

the ground. The plants were then laid upon the ground, and left thus upon the land until the next day, care being observed that no damage was done by cold during the night. By this process the leaves—which, in their growing state, are more or less brittle—became limp and wilted, so that they could be handled with less risk of damage.

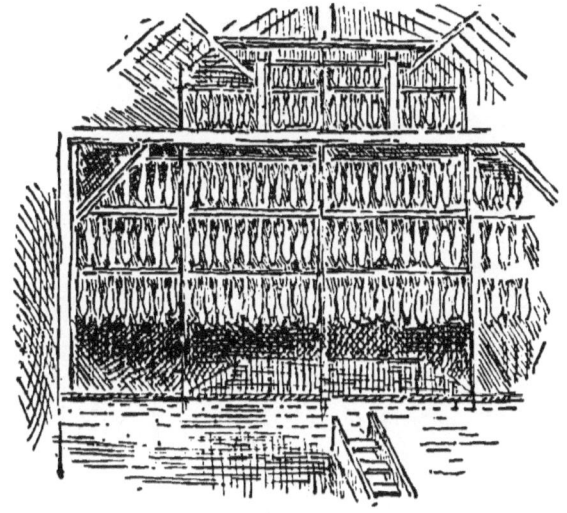

SECTION SHOWING INTERIOR OF BARN USED IN CURING MESSRS. CARTERS' TOBACCO.

A second group of men made incisions at the thick end of the stem; whilst others, again, threaded the plants—averaging about six plants to a hazel rod—upon rods, specially prepared. These, in their turn, were carried to the waggon, as shown in the illustration on the preceding page.

F

The plants were then carted to the barn, and after the tobacco upon each rod had been weighed, they were suspended as shown in the illustration on page 65, great care being taken that the plants did not touch each other, either upon the rods or in the tiers.

CURING MESSRS. CARTERS' TOBACCO.

The curing of the plants commenced immediately the housing of the crop was completed, and the process is admitted to have progressed satisfactorily, although the conditions were not by any means the most favourable, inasmuch as no adequate provision had been made for the proper "firing" of the Tobacco; in fact, it was found necessary to use an ordinary barn hired near the growing crop for this special purpose, very exposed and not proof against the weather, as the only available structure, whilst it was quite impracticable for upwards of five weeks to "fire" the crop (in consequence of the difficulties of insurance), a process highly necessary during wet weather.

Instead of this treatment, the first stages of "curing" were by cold air. This operation is at all times accompanied by a considerable amount of risk of damage to the leaf by mildew and decay, as well as being much slower than the "firing" system.

These imperfect conditions will, however, be easily overcome in the future, and the simple preparations requisite for the proper curing of the crop will doubtless be provided by those who continue these interesting experiments.

It has already been stated that the first stages in curing the Tobacco were confined to "cold" drying only. This process consisted in a most careful daily watching of the atmospheric conditions; thus, during the prevalence of dry easterly winds or cold bright weather generally, the freest possible ventilation was given, the barn doors being opened fully, so that the wind could play directly upon the Tobacco. In moist, foggy, or humid weather, on the contrary, the doors were kept as close as possible, and contact with the outside air avoided. This treatment was continued for nearly five weeks, *i.e.*, until about October 25th, when the difficulties of fire insurance were surmounted, and the first fire lighted; and not one day too soon did these changed conditions take place, the weather of the last ten days or a fortnight before fires were used being remarkably damp and foggy, and the Tobacco began to show unmistakable signs of mildew. At the same time undue haste in firing cannot be recommended; in fact, several experts who have given very pronounced opinions upon the superiority of the Tobacco produced by Messrs. Carter, as compared with examples differently treated, expressed a decided opinion that the excellent quality of this Tobacco was largely due to the slow process of curing; and except in cases where bright golden colour in the leaf is aimed at rather than smoking quality, it is deemed desirable to *cold air dry* the Tobacco, say for a fortnight or three weeks if the weather is fine and dry; if on the other hand the air is wet and the atmosphere heavy, then slow firing should be commenced at once. By slow firing it is meant that a sufficient heat should be produced to dry up any atmospheric moisture entering the building, and also to absorb a certain quantity of that exuded from the leaves and stems of the Tobacco.

Messrs. Carters' Tobacco was submitted to this treatment, and a moderate "firing" as suggested above was continued for about a month.

Eventually, on or about November 25th, the Tobacco, which in the process of drying had already shrunk in bulk quite fifty per cent., was packed close in the tiers, and canvas walls were constructed to make the area as confined as possible, and thus to increase the temperature. By this process an average range of day heat of from 80 to 90 degrees was obtained and continued for four or five days, when the Tobacco was considered sufficiently cured to be taken down and "handed" as described at pages 72–77.

The apparatus for heating the barn; as shown here :

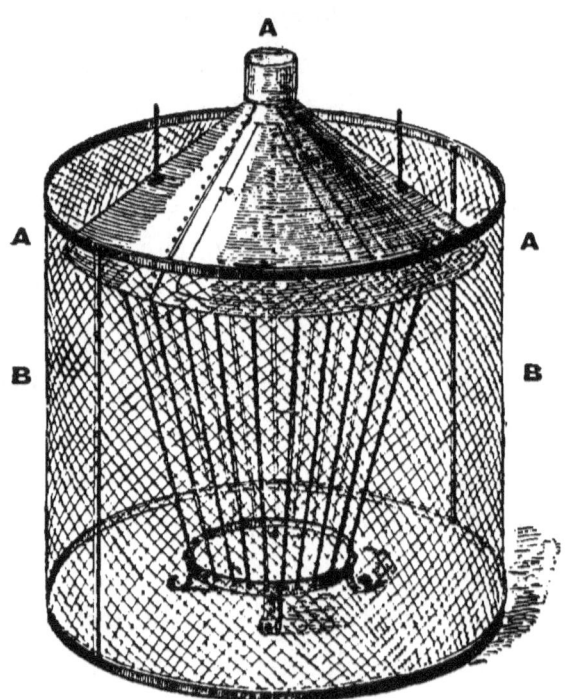

CARTERS' TOBACCO FURNACE (*Registered*).

suggested itself to Messrs. Carter as serving the required object under circumstances that rendered a naked fire utterly impossible, the barn being a huge wooden building in the centre of cow-sheds, stables, stacks, etc., that must have been destroyed had a fire taken possession of the barn.

In the first place the furnace was portable, and thus could if necessary be readily moved; secondly, wood of any and every description could be consumed in the furnace, and the novel "cap" or umbrella-shaped dome (A), combined with the side-guards (B), was successful in checking the escape of sparks and flame, whilst the peculiar formation of the dome assisted in the distribution of heat. (Particulars of the Tobacco Furnace can be obtained of Messrs. Carter.)

"HANDING" & FINISHING MESSRS. CARTERS' TOBACCO FOR MARKET.

The accompanying Illustration gives an excellent idea of the process of "handing" the Tobacco—*i.e.*, stripping the leaves from the stalks, and tying them into bundles of a given number of leaves.

The Tobacco being pronounced sufficiently dry, or cured, the fire is put out, and the outside air freely admitted. This precaution, after high firing, is most important, as the Tobacco, in the process of drying, becomes so brittle that at the slightest touch it crumbles into a snuff-like condition. The object of a free circulation of air is to soften the leaf, and render it pliable and easy to handle. This condition—known by Americans as "in case"—will be produced in a day or two, according to the weather, after firing has ceased, when the

"HANDING" AND FINISHING THE TOBACCO.

Tobacco should appear to the touch more like thin kid leather than anything else to which it may be compared.

STRIPPING AND HANDING MESSRS. CARTERS' TOBACCO.

The above process is an important feature, as bearing upon the value of the manufactured article, it being the special duty of the individual removing the leaves from the plant (*see Illustration*) to sort them when stripped into three qualities, familiarly known in America as *Lugs*, i.e., those leaves nearest the ground, usually more or less damaged; *Firsts*, the brightest and best coloured leaves; and *Seconds*, the medium quality leaves; and it will, in a great measure, depend upon how this sorting is done to determine the market value of the whole of the produce. It is, however, an art easily gained after a little experience; and a knowledge of the proper selection of the leaves is acquired after a lesson or two from some one who is familiar with the operation.

"Handing" the Tobacco consists of the leaves being picked up from the table by women and children (*see Illustration*), the *butt* ends being neatly placed together, and the number determined upon—from twelve to twenty leaves—being neatly bound round with another leaf of the same kind, the end being secured by insertion between the leaves.

After the hands are "tied" or "bound," as already described, they are passed through the closed hand of the workers, to bring the Tobacco into a smaller compass; this is repeated several times as the hands are passed from one worker to the next, and ultimately to the packer, who carefully piles the "hands" of Tobacco into a solid block, composed of the width of two hands, the butts coming to the outside of the pile, and the tips of the leaves to the centre. In this manner the Tobacco is packed into a small compass, the usual size of the piles being about six feet in length by three feet in depth when trodden down by the packer, care being taken to have the floor, upon which the Tobacco is laid, quite clean.

With the object of pressing the Tobacco in bulk as much as possible, each layer, as the heap enlarges, is trodden firm in the centre by the packer, who usually wears a pair of slippers during the operation, so that no dirt may become mixed with the Tobacco.

This process of treading assists the more rapid fermentation of the Tobacco, which is the object sought to be gained by packing down.

It is in this process of fermentation that the greatest care is necessary to avoid over-heating, and the bulk must be examined occasionally to guard against such a calamity; if, upon examination, the heat appears to be excessive, the safest plan is to pull the stack to pieces, let it cool down, and then re-bulk it. Any extra trouble taken with the Tobacco in this stage will be amply repaid by its superior condition, and ultimately by the increased market value over produce less carefully handled.

The Tobacco when in this condition should if possible be disposed of to the manufacturer (or to the depôt, such as it is hoped will be forthcoming in various agricultural centres, as the cultivation becomes more general), who will (as in France under the Régie Nationale) undertake its development through the second fermentation in spring, familiarly designated as the "May sweat" by Americans.

This is the final stage, and after such fermentation it is usual in foreign Tobacco producing centres for the crop to be packed into cases or hogsheads, and sent into the market.

It will, however, be remembered that at the period at which this work was written (January, 1887) it was impossible to pursue such treatment; and as Messrs. Carters' Tobacco passed into the hands of the manufacturers in December, 1886, records of "Spring" treatment must be reserved for later editions of this work.

The successful culture of Tobacco may be summed up in a very few words: Attentive observation of the rules laid down by English experimentalists, rather than attempting to follow the customs of other nations, which are frequently impossible or undesirable in this country; and the exercise of daily observation, which will often suggest some improved system of procedure. The concluding words of an interesting paper, written by an American, upon the subject of Tobacco, are worthy of repetition here: "If you have not a large stock of patience and perseverance, with a will to learn, and a resolution to keep trying until you succeed, you have missed your calling, and had better try something else. For there is no royal road to success in Tobacco raising. But if you possess the true essentials—have the true and lasting pluck—you will succeed soon, or late, and what is better, reap a full reward for honest, faithful toil."

ANALYSIS.

We are favoured with the following report of an analysis—so far as completed—of our Tobacco, now being conducted by Dr. Bell, at the Laboratory, Inland Revenue, Somerset House, but which was not perfected at the time of going to press.

VIRGINIA (*partly cured*).
Nicotine . 4·2 per cent.
*Ash . . 21·7 per cent.
* Nearly a maximum.

ISLAND BROADLEAF (*nearly cured*).
Nicotine . 2·6 per cent.

NOTE.—In Imported Virginian Tobacco the average analysis gives:

Nicotine . . . 3·0 per cent.
Ash . . . 18·0 pe cent.

CONTINENTAL TOBACCO CULTURE.

WITH BALANCE-SHEET OF BELGIAN CROPS.

At the present moment we import large quantities of Tobacco from Holland, Hungary, Germany, and France, while in former years in England, Scotland, and Ireland it was successfully cultivated till the law stepped in and put an end to the practice.

Brodigan, a successful Tobacco-grower in Ireland fifty years ago, says, with regard to the climate: " It is well-known that as we approach the tropics the calamities to which vegetation is subject increase. Whereas in our uniform climate we are exempt from those devastating hurricanes, hailstorms, inundations, and periodical gales, which in a few moments destroy the hopes of the planter, etc." He continues to enumerate the diseases and injuries to which the plant is subject in Virginia, *i.e.*, "wormholes, ripeshot or sunburnt, moonburnt, houseburnt, or stunted by growth, torn by storms of hail or wind, injured or killed by frosts," while in the British Isles, except for an occasional gale or late frost, we are free from these dangers.

On the Continent Tobacco is a State Monopoly; the State fixes its own profits, and all Tobacco is carried to depôts, where regular commissioners give the planters a fair market price. The Belgian system differs, however, and to their simple and efficacious method reference is made further on.

As far as allotments or small holdings are concerned, the cultivation of Tobacco would be apparently the only means of making such a system a profitable one, as will be shown in the case of Belgium.

Tobacco growing can be practised and made profitable on exceedingly small areas of land and without the outlay of much capital, the *sine quâ non* being the employment of a great deal of manual labour.

The following very interesting and valuable facts

have been obtained from Belgian cultivators of Tobacco :

COST OF TOBACCO PRODUCTION PER HECTARE
(1 HECTARE = 2 ACRES 1 ROD 1 POLE) FOR ONE YEAR.

	Francs.	£
1. Various manures	1,000	= 40
2. Labour approximately	1,000	= 40
3. Government tax, 2 centimes (one-fifth of a penny) per plant; about 40,000 plants per hectare	800	= 32
4. Rent, rates, taxes	300	= 12
Total outlay	3,100	= £124

The Government tax of 2 cents. the plant, which is levied on the standing crop, is not exacted on useless plants.

Produce of 1 hectare : An ordinary year readily yields a production of 3,000 kilogrammes per hectare (1 kilo = 2 lb. 3¼ oz.), of which 70 per cent. is of first quality, and 30 per cent. of second and third quality; these inferior qualities sell at 20 per cent. less; the first quality is selling at present at :

	Francs.
1 franc 50 cents. (1s. 3d.) per kilo, or for 2,100 kilos...	3,150
2nd and 3rd qualities, selling at 1 franc, or for 900 kilos	900
	4,050
The expenses being...	3,100
The net profit is (£38)	950

In this calculation it must not be forgotten—first, that Belgian rates are far higher than our own; second, that the cost of manures has been put down at an exorbitant rate; third, that in accounting for the manure, a margin, and a large one, must be left to the good, in consideration of the benefit derived by the succeeding crops, of which four or five can be taken off the same land without any fresh addition; and, fourth, that the Belgian authorities declare that the above calculation holds good with the *small* landowners who now exclusively carry on the cultivation to the employment of their whole families, but who cannot use enough manure to be able to procure it at wholesale prices. In this, and in other instances, cultivation on a large scale would ensure much larger relative receipts.

A capital of from 500 to 700 francs per hectare is considered necessary for building the thatched drying-sheds and pine-poles for curing purposes.

Reprinted from "AGRICULTURE," April 14, 1886.

A REPORT ON THE GROWTH OF TOBACCO ON A QUARTER OF AN ACRE OF LAND ON LORD WALSINGHAM'S HOME FARM AT MERTON, NORFOLK, IN 1886.

THE land upon which the tobacco was grown may be described as fairly good mixed light land with a sandy subsoil, the agricultural rental value of which may, in ordinary times, be estimated at about 22s. per acre for rent and tithe.

The preparation for the tobacco plant was as follows: The land was twice ploughed, the depth of the first ploughing was 6 in. and the second 7 in. deep. The land was harrowed after each ploughing, and especially after the second earth, when it was well worked to get a good and fine tilth. It was then ridged up into balks 30 in. apart, and six full-sized cartloads of well-made farmyard manure was put on to the quarter of an acre of land. After the manure was applied the ridges were split down by a double breast plough, which effectually covered the manure. A light wood roll was run over the ridges to level them, and also to pulverise the soil to receive the tobacco plants.

On June 16 last the plants were received from Carter & Co. in good fresh condition, and were carefully planted the same day. The number of each variety of tobacco plant was as follows: Big Frederick, 100; Virginia, 100; Pennsylvania, 1,100; Connecticut, 400—total 1,700.

For about three weeks after planting the weather was very dry and cold, and the plants appeared to make no progress, but rather went backward than forward, although the precaution was taken to put sheepfold cloths, supported by hurdles, to protect them from the cold north winds prevailing at that time.

It was recommended that a pinch of gypsum should be put on the crown of each plant, and that they should not be watered. It was seen that the plants made no progress; therefore, against the advice received, they were watered on the first and third days of July, and from that time the leaves freshened and the plants made a rapid and vigorous growth. The land about the plants was carefully hand-hoed three or four times, and between the balks it was deeply cultivated.

On Aug. 10, the side shoots on the plants were pinched off, and this was done every time they appeared. On the 19th of the same month, or within a few days following this date, the leading shoots of the plants were removed, leaving about nine of the best leaves on each plant. It is desirable that it should be known that it is important that the leading shoots of each plant should be stopped, for while the leaves on a few left unchecked were about 18 in. long and 7 in. wide, many of the leaves on the plants where the leading shoots were removed were 36 in. long and 18 in. wide.

In consequence of the appearance of frost, it was thought advisable to secure the crop, and therefore the plants were cut off close to the ground on Sept. 20; but before this was done, the stalks were split open from the top to about 2 in. from the bottom. The plants were then carefully placed across sticks, each stick being 4 ft. long, and carrying eight plants. The sticks upon which the plants were hung were then carried to the drying houses. In about a week's time from the plants being hung up in the drying houses wood fires were kept burning during the day and part of the night, and the temperature was kept as nearly as possible at 70° for about fourteen days, when it was raised to about 80°. When the plants were first placed in the houses, they necessarily occupied more space than they did when the leaves withered. The plants were afterwards placed close together. The fires were kept going until all the sap disappeared from the stems and from the middle rib of the leaves. For the last two days of the fires being used the temperature of the sheds was raised to 90°. After this the plants were left hanging to allow the leaves to relax, so that they could be stripped from the stems, sorted, and tied into bundles, each bundle containing, say, eight leaves, which were neatly bound together at the top by a half leaf. After the leaves were bound as described above, the bundles—or hands, as they are called in America—were packed closely together on boards, and covered with sacks and weighted, the temperature of the room being kept sufficiently high to prevent mould.

From THE FIELD, *December* 18*th*, 1886.

A REPORT ON THE GROWTH OF TOBACCO ON A QUARTER OF AN ACRE OF LAND ON SIR E. BIRKBECK'S HOME FARM AT HORSTEAD, NORFOLK.

"*Experientia docet* is one of the principles of Sir Edward Birkbeck's political life. Sir Edward resolved to ascertain by experiments, carried out under his own eye at Horstead, whether or not he had asked for a concession from Her Majesty's Government which was likely to be of advantage to the English agriculturists. Though the season was late for making the experiment, he determined to plant two plots of land at Horstead with several varieties of tobacco. One plot was situated in the kitchen garden alongside a bed of asparagus; another plot at the end of an open and exposed field on which barley was growing. There had been no special cultivation of either plot for this particular plant, which had to take its chance in the kitchen garden with the vegetables for culinary use, and in the field with the barley crop. But it may be inferred that the land in each case was in 'good heart,' though not in such excellent condition as is considered by many necessary for tobacco cultivation.

"The seeds were sown in a hotbed, where they grew rapidly, and then pricked out in shallow wooden boxes to be kept for a time in a lower temperature. It was not till the middle of June, because of the cold nights which would be fatal to them, that the plants could be set out in the open ground.

"There were six rows of as many varieties of *Nicotiana* in the kitchen garden at Horstead. The first, *Nicotiana rustica*, a Turkish tobacco. The seed was sown on 18th April, and the plants were set out 15 inches apart in the open on 18th June, though they were ready for removal out-doors earlier had the weather been favourable. The plants grew about a foot high and appeared stunted. Clearly *it is not so well adapted* as other varieties to the English climate. Alongside this variety was a row of *N. Texana* also sown on 18th April, and planted out 15 inches apart on 18th June. The plants attained a height of from 3 feet to 3 feet 3 inches, and bore fine leaves, some as large as 10½ inches by 12 inches. Next came *N. Syriana*, sown on 18th April and planted out 15 inches apart on 19th June. Irregular in height throughout, though there were several good plants with leaves varying from 10 inches by 14 inches to 14 inches by 15 inches. *N. Lebanon*, the next variety, was sown on 18th April, and planted out 2 feet 6 inches apart on 18th June ; but the plants had partly died off, while the leaves left were spotted. *N. Virginia* was the finest show. The seeds were sown on 15th April, and the young plants set out 2 feet 3 inches apart on 18th June. The experiment has shown that it would have been better had the space between the plants been greater. The plants were about 3 feet high, and each bore ten or a dozen leaves about 2 feet 6 inches long by 10 or 11 inches broad. This is undoubtedly the variety which thrives best. *N. attenuata*, sown and planted the same time as the other varieties, had done fairly well, though the growth was somewhat uneven. Some of the leaves measured 13 inches by 24 inches.

"Next we inspected the plot in the barley field, where the same varieties were planted in patches of four or five short rows. There the same characteristics were displayed—the Western varieties were larger and more luxuriant than the Eastern. The Virginian variety in the barley field appeared more vigorous than that in the kitchen garden, as the long leaves stood erect, while the colour of the leaf looked better.

This may be owing to the difference in the manuring of the soil. The Government will be asked to give their sanction to the continuance of the experiments another year, and to afford greater facilities for conducting them. No doubt the request will be granted. In that case Sir Edward Birkbeck intends continuing his experiments next year, upon soil specially prepared, with the varieties which have proved to be the most luxuriant. The plants of course require much attention. All the flower panicles are picked off as they appear, so that the growth may be diverted into the leaf. The Inland Revenue officers have paid particular attention to the development of the plants, and reports have been made from time to time on the progress of the experiments. Samples of earth in which the plants grow have also been sent up to those who have supervision of the several experiments now being conducted in the country."—*Anon.*

The following particulars are furnished by Messrs. Carters' Expert, who "handled" this crop and prepared it for market:

"At maturity the *Turkish* and *Syriana* were not equal in size of leaf or quality to either the *Texana*, *Attenuata*, or *Virginia*, in fact were evidently not adapted to the climate. The *Texana* was fair tobacco, but not equal to the *Attenuata* or *Virginia*, both of which varieties were good, the Virginia especially having very large leaves, many of which would have had more body had the plants been topped sooner. The growth of the two last-named varieties must convince even the most prejudiced that tobacco can be grown, and profitably so, in the Eastern counties; that, together with the fact of tobacco having been grown in Scotland, ought to remove all existing doubts as to its successful cultivation throughout the British Isles."

A REPORT UPON A QUARTER OF AN ACRE OF TOBACCO

GROWN IN KENT BY

C. DE LAUNE FAUNCE DE LAUNE, Esq., J.P.

The soil varies at Lynsted, part of the district being poor, shallow, and stony. There were several plots of tobacco, of many varieties, and although here and there was a belt of favouritism noticeable, the general overlook satisfied the eye that all sorts had fairly succeeded. It was not a case of success in one plot and failure in another; simply, varieties showed themselves varieties; some liked the soil and the character of the manures underneath them better than did their neighbours. This rule was not restricted to the "common" sorts, for some of the best varieties were also most "at home" at Lynsted. Farmyard manures, wood ashes, and sheep droppings had been applied to the ground, from which hops had been grubbed up. Mr. de Laune raised some of his plants from seed placed in a hotbed during May, and set out from June 10 to June 26. Other plots were from seedling plants reared by Messrs. Carter, of Holborn. The distance of the plants apart is about a yard—as recommended by American practice—but the luxuriance of the English plants demands much more space for the large-leaved varieties, so as to allow room between the rows to cultivate and clean the crop from rapidly-growing suckers, etc. This work could not possibly be accomplished without a greater evil following, through injury to the finely-grown and ripening leaves overlapping each other.

ENGLISH TOBACCO CULTURE.

In reply to a schedule of questions, Mr. de Laune has favoured me with the following particulars:

1. Names of varieties grown: Kentucky, Connecticut, Pennsylvania, Island Broadleaf, Hester, Virginia, etc.
2. Prepared bed for plants with foot of farmyard manure and a few inches of loam on the top. Did not burn over the soil before planting out. Covered the seed plants with sheets on cold nights.
3. Set out plants (June 10 to 26) in hills made by hand.
4. Percentage of first planting which rooted and grew off. Very few died from natural causes, and none from insects or worms.
5. The soil is loamy (formerly a hop garden); last crop turnips, fed off by sheep.
6. Manures: Wood ashes, bats' guano, farmyard muck, etc. How applied: Direct to the plant hills and broadcast.
8. Date of first topping, July 24. Average number of leaves left on each plant to mature, 10. I did not prime or pull off inferior leaves.
9. Did not see any horn worm.
10. Earwigs the only insects that preyed upon the plants.
11. Daily record of weather.—Refer for this to district tables.
12. Costs of producing crop. Must have time to answer.
13. Date of cutting.—Commenced September 3 and September 22. Mode of curing.—By fires in hop oasts.
14. Total yield in pounds of marketable tobacco per acre, and in what proportions of quality.—Answer must be postponed.

The tobacco leaves as they were cut were strung together in pairs, and at once suspended from a rod supported by a newly-made wooden horse nearly two feet broad, and over a yard in length, the right height, so the leaves cleared the ground, and when the rod was completed it was carried away to a framework on wheels, which latter when loaded, was trundled off to the ample oast-house. This picking of the leaves, for curing, rather than straddle the whole plants in pairs, seemed to me decidedly the best practice, as the stalks require much more time and heat to dry than do the leaves. At the oast-house I made my first acquaintance with dried English tobacco in various stages. At Lynsted the smokeless coal of the oast-house fires gives out plenty of heat (laden with sulphurous fumes), yet I could not see well how the crescendo scale of temperature could be regulated with a delicacy necessary to the process. Some Kentucky leaves had been very successfully treated; the yellow colour was as true as a lady's fawn-coloured glove, and the pliability and suppleness were much the same; but next comes the task of fixing this colour, and at present this work has to be accomplished. Besides, the good yellows frequently go off into the quiet brown colour seen in our best cigars. It is as smoking tobacco, for pipes and cigarettes, that the yellow colour commands a high price. Having already made tentative efforts with a small portion of his crop, Mr. de Laune will start well in his undertaking to cure the bulk of the crop. Tiers of light rods are stretching across the oast-house, intermediate and row above row, ready to receive the freshly charged rods of leaves or plants as they come from the drying-rooms over the fires. I noted amongst various samples some common Massachusetts plants, which to me seemed satisfactorily cured without any artificial heat, having been simply hung under cover in a current of air. These were of a dark leathery brown colour. Each step taken is an experience indicating how best to advance, and in this single season mistakes may be considered but as stepping-stones towards future success.—MR. KAINS-JACKSON *in the Farmers' Almanack*, 1887.

TOBACCO CULTIVATION IN IRELAND, 1886.

The following interesting reports describe two satisfactory attempts at Tobacco *growing* in Ireland, although the course of treatment of the leaves when grown was not always of the most desirable character. For example: Mr. Wallace, at p. 93, describes how he made the *green leaves* into *hands*, and at p. 94 he admits the mistake thus made. These and similar experiences go to prove the necessity felt for a reliable and permanent guide to Tobacco Culture such as, it is hoped, this little volume is destined to supply.

C. J. Wallace, Esq., writes as follows:

"I raised my stock from seed supplied from James Carter & Co. The seed was sown in pans in the hothouse, and by degrees the plants were hardened off in a cold greenhouse. They were next pricked out simply in a light mild litter. When the weather got settled about the end of May the plants were put out about twenty inches apart, in richly-manured ground, in a sheltered situation and sunny aspect, on raised drills, about twenty or twenty-four inches apart. They grew to a great size, and required much care in nipping off the shoots from time to time, as I think my drills were too close together. (In future I would plant further apart, as I found there was a liability to injure the leaves in passing through.) It is better to plant too far apart than too close, I believe, and one cannot be too careful and constant about the nipping of the young shoots. I did not begin to gather my crop until September, and did the work only on fine days when all was dry.

"(1) *First*, I *singly gathered* a large quantity of the leaves which I considered matured, and though the process was tedious, I had them tied together in couples and suspended on string across light, airy rooms. These were only the largest and most matured leaves, selected, so to say, as specimens.

"(2) Next, a little later on, I *cut at the roots* some hundreds of the plants that had the finest leaves—say about a dozen, more or less, on each plant—and nailed them as they were, point downwards, to the rafters of sheds and out-houses, lofts, etc., with long French nails. I found this a simple and easy process, as, when desirable, the plants could be easily removed if damp showed, and put in some more airy and light position to dry in.

"(3) My third process was to gather direct from the remaining plants as they stood all those leaves which seemed matured and of a solid texture, leaving ungathered (for I had not room to hang all my crop) any leaves that seemed flabby and thin. These I made into the orthodox 'hands' of, say eight to twelve leaves, bound round the butt ends with one leaf and secured in the ordinary way of growers. These hands were hung on lines as were the first lot of leaves gathered. All the crop remained hanging until the leaves had turned a uniform yellow tone of colour and fairly dry. I then collected the (1) first, and placed the leaves one over the other in piles of about a foot high, each leaf smoothed and slightly pressed out.

"I packed them then fairly tight together in baskets, and covered all with carpets and such things. They remained thus for about a month while I was from home. They were, I am told really *heated* so as to get moist, or 'sweated;' still, they got of a fine rich colour and good texture when they came to be opened out.

"(2) The plants of the second lot (those nailed by stems to rafters, etc.) were taken down singly, and the leaves removed and treated like the first lot of leaves that were gathered from the young plants. I consider the texture and quality of these latter leaves, which dried on the stem, are superior in most ways (except colour) to the leaves which were removed from stems before dry.

"(3) My third gathering of leaves which were tied in 'hands' were by no means so successful in curing as the other lots. They were more liable to damp and moisture, and the colour was not nearly so good; in fact, the whole lot has still a green tinge through it, but their having been gathered late in the season may partially account for this. However, I do not believe that our climate (especially in Ireland) will admit of drying tobacco when hung in 'hands.' I believe the leaves will have to be kept quite separate so that the air may get through them, or they will not cure properly.

"My opinion is, the best plan is to cut the plants and hang to dry as I did with No. 2 lot, and when the plants have got a good colour and are fairly dry, remove leaves in 'hands' or singly, and finish the process. My tobacco is of a moist, excellent flavour and aroma, but remarkably *strong*. I have made up some into cigars, and, as far as I can at present judge for such fresh stuff, it is A.1. tobacco, but, as I said, strong. As pipe-smoking tobacco it is stronger still, so that if I make another experiment next year I shall get seed of the mildest kind I can procure, for I fancy the damp climate here has something to say to the strength of leaves. They would be more sappy than if grown in a dry, warmer climate, and therefore stronger in flavour.

"CHARLES J. WALLACE."

Belfield, Co. Dublin,
    Jan. 15, 1887.

THE following report is kindly furnished by L. McCORMICK, ESQ.:

"As soon as I became aware that the Lords of the Treasury had given permission for the experimental growing of Tobacco,

CULTIVATION IN IRELAND. 95

I was desirous of taking up the culture of the plant as a field crop. I gave notice to the Secretary of Inland Revenue, Somerset House, of my intention, stating that I would plant a rood.

"Not knowing which were the most suitable sorts to grow, I wrote to Messrs. Carter, asking them to forward me a few packets of seed for trial, upon which they sent Connecticut and Havana varieties. It was then the second week in May, and being so far advanced in the season, I almost gave up the idea of attempting the task. However, late as it was, I knew I could learn something, and so determined to make a trial. I sowed the seeds in gentle heat on a hotbed under glass, and in about two weeks I had quite two thousand nice little plants, from the two packets of seed, ready for pricking out.

"About this time I received a letter from the Secretary of Inland Revenue stating that, as the farm on which I purposed growing the tobacco was so far from the officer's residence, the Board of Inland Revenue would not allow me to grow any. However, after some correspondence, they at length gave me permission towards the end of June.

"Having been delayed so long, I pricked off only a portion of the seedlings into shallow boxes, two and a half inches apart, resolving to make a trial at any risk, even though I were obliged to destroy the crop. I prepared a portion of a field (somewhat less than a rood), manured it, and set out the drills three feet apart.

"By the second week of June the little plants grew fairly strong, and after exposing them to the open air for a few days, I transferred the boxes of Tobacco plants to the field.

"First I rolled the drills to make the soil firm, and then had the plants transferred from the boxes by cutting them out in squares without disturbing their roots. I next planted them in drills with a trowel two and a half feet apart. After a few waterings the plants grew freely.

"The attention the crop afterwards received was that of hand-hoeing, horse-hoeing, and grubbing, at intervals, until the plants grew too large for horses to pass between the drills. By the beginning of August the plants had grown so much that they could not be got through easily without injuring them, some of the leaves of the Connecticut variety measuring more than three feet in length and one foot in breadth. I found I did not give them enough room. About this time the flower heads appeared, and I topped the plants, leaving from eight to ten leaves on each. Afterwards I had the laterals disbudded as they appeared, or about once a week until the last week in September, when I got the whole crop cut and conveyed in farm carts to the drying-rooms, taking the precaution of placing the plants in regular order lest they should get injured. They were unloaded carefully, hung up in the drying-rooms by their lower ends, and dried and cured by means of stoves and pipes. The temperature of the rooms never exceeded eighty degrees, nor do I think a higher temperature would have answered so well under the circumstances, as I observed those plants that were subject to the greatest heat came out green when dried, whereas those that dried out gradually were of a light brown colour.

"Nearly six weeks elapsed from the time the crop was gathered in till it was perfectly dry and fit for packing. I submitted samples to some of the leading manufacturers in Dublin and other parts of Ireland. They have all spoken in favourable terms of it. The whole of the produce (206 lbs.) has been bought by Messrs. P. J. Carroll & Co., of Dundalk, at sixpence per pound.

"Although my experiment has not proved a financial success, I feel quite pleased at the result. I am convinced that tobacco can be grown and cured successfully in Ireland; and now, I suppose, it only remains for us, with the consent of the 'powers that be,' to learn how to grow it profitably.

"L. McCORMICK."

Rowleston House,
   Kilsallaghan,
      Co. Dublin.

THE CULTIVATION OF TOBACCO
IN
STOCKHOLM.

By M. FORSSELL.

As the main object of Tobacco cultivation in the surroundings of Stockholm is to produce large quantities rather than fine quality, they manure the ground very liberally, viz., 50,000 to 60,000 kilograms (50 to 60 tons) per half hectar ($1\frac{1}{4}$ statute acres) of well-decayed manure. The manuring generally takes place during the winter and early spring, after which the field is ploughed and harrowed in case of necessity once, and sometimes twice. After this there are drills laid up about four feet distant from each other, their surface being finely pulverised and levelled down, and the positions of the plants marked out with a string, allowing an intervening space of two feet. Upon the drills are planted two lines of tobacco plants, two feet between each plant in the line.

The plants, which have to be strong and vigorous, are prepared in medium warm hotbeds and transplanted in the end of May and beginning of June, when no sharp, frosty nights are to be apprehended. During the month of June the tobacco culture is reduced to replanting of withered plants, and cleansing and laying earth round the stem of the plants after they have five to six leaves, the largest being about six inches long. After the earth has been laid round the stem of the plants they grow very quickly, and in the middle of July the gathering of the sandgoods, *i.e.*, the three to five lowest leaves on every stalk, commences. These leaves would if left on the stalk be yellow and of no value, as the upper leaves would take the light away; they are consequently gathered and brought into the barn, where the middle nerve of the leaf or rib is cloven and removed from about a quarter or a half of an inch from the point of the leaf-stalk to about the third of the length of the leaf. Afterwards the leaves are hung on sticks to dry. It is necessary to leave a little space between each leaf, as damp weather would make them mouldy, which would lessen their value.

At the end of the gathering of the "Sandgoods," *i.e.*, bottom leaves, all buds and stems coming in the upper leaf wrinkles are carefully taken away. During the rest of the time the plant has to vegetate (the harvesting of the large leaves is executed between the 20th of August and 20th of September), it must be seen that the remainder of the leaves are developed as completely as possible. The plant is topped as soon as the buds commence to show themselves, all stalks growing in the leaf wrinkles are carefully plucked. Dealt with in that way, all the sap of nourishment goes to the leaves. The crop is generally topped so low that only seven to ten leaves are left; these leaves, which are called the "Largegoods," are gathered and dried in the same way as the "Sandgoods."

About two months after the suspending of the leaves (this greatly depending upon the weather) the leaves are dry. On a rainy or damp day, when the leaves feel soft, the sticks are taken down, the leaves are removed and put into bundles of about two to four kilograms weight, after which the tobacco is *immediately delivered to the tobacco factories, where the sweating takes place*, and before which operation the leaves cannot be used. The sweating lasts several months, and it is very few Stockholm tobacco cultivators that undertake this operation.

The harvest product per half hectar ($1\frac{1}{4}$ statute acres) varies considerably, of course depending upon the qualification of the earth, the temperature of the summer, and proportion of rain.

The crop is generally reckoned to give from 850 to 1,275 kilograms per half hectar, and as the "Sandgoods" is valued at 6½d. per kilogram, and the "Largegoods" at 9d. per kilogram, the gross production comes to from £34 to £45 per half a hectar.

THE TOBACCO WORM.
(Sphinx quinquemaculatus.)

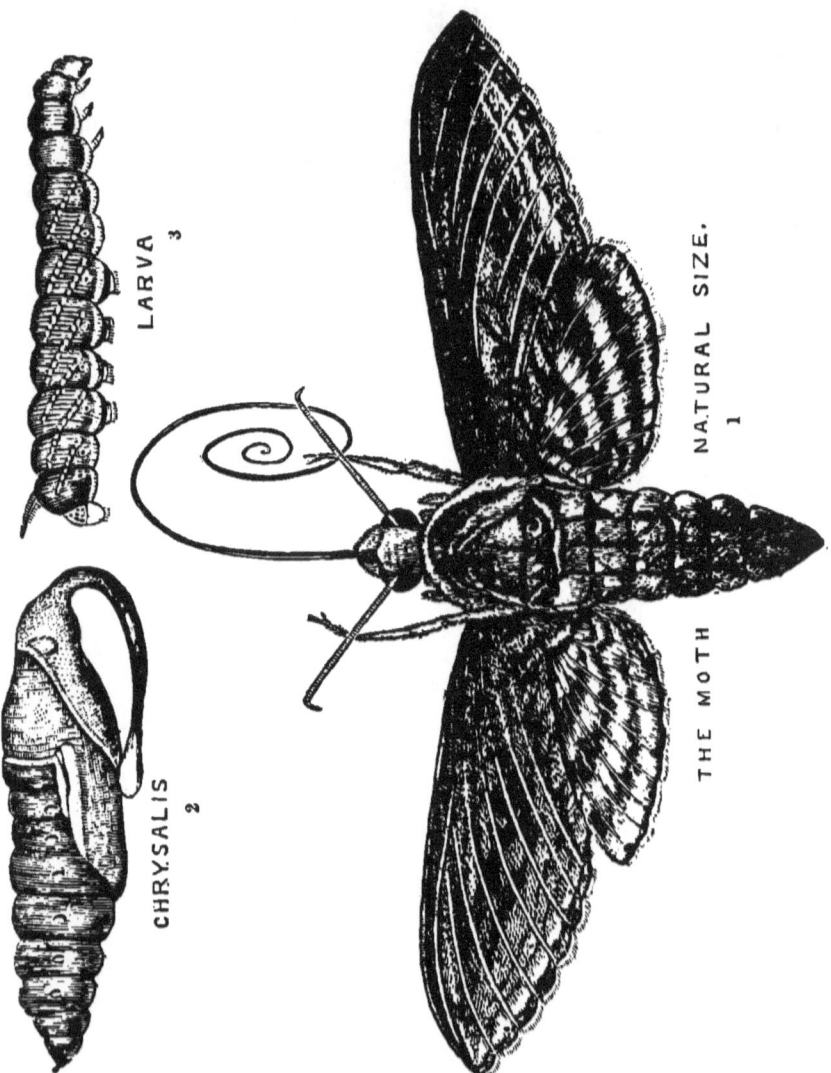

No. 1 drawn from a specimen in Messrs. Carters' Laboratory, 237 & 238, High Holborn, London.

The above engraving represents one of the most voracious and destructive insects that the American Tobacco, Potatoe, and

THE TOBACCO WORM.

Tomato crops has to contend with—happily it is unknown in England at present. It is shown in its different stages of larva, chrysalis, and imago, or moth. The larva or worm (see fig. 3) is a great pest upon Potatoe and Tomato vines, and upon Tobacco. It is especially injurious to the latter crop, as it perforates the leaves and renders them ragged and worthless. The worm as it comes from the egg is so small as to be unobserved, but having an enormous appetite, it devours rapidly, and soon grows to about twice the size represented in the cut. When not feeding, it lifts up the head and fore-part of the body, and remains apparently lifeless. From its resemblance in this position to the Egyptian Sphinx, Linnæus gave the name *Sphinx* to the genus. The larva is of a light green colour, with whitish oblique stripes, and has a horn upon the rear end of the body. Though it is repulsive in appearance, it is perfectly harmless to touch, and may be picked off with the hands without fear. After it has reached its full size, it leaves the scene of its ravages and goes into the earth, where it throws off its skin and becomes a brown-coloured chrysalis (see fig. 2). The curious projection, like a handle, is a sheath which holds the tongue of the future moth. The moth, or perfect insect, is represented in the engraving (see fig. 1), of the natural size, and is reproduced here from a specimen on view in Messrs. Carters' Laboratory, High Holborn. It is of a grey colour, with orange-coloured spots on each side of the body. As there are five of these spots on each side, it is called *Sphinx quinquemaculatus*, or Five-spotted Sphinx. In America the moths may be seen towards night flitting about the flowers, from which they suck the juices by means of their remarkable tongue, which is five or six inches long. When the tongue is not in use, it is closely coiled up and hidden between the two feelers. From the manner of their flight and feeding they are frequently mistaken for humming-birds and are called "humming-bird moths," and "horn-blowers." The moths should always be destroyed if possible; by so doing, the production of several hundreds of most destructive worms is prevented.

Naturalists make one or two other species, which closely resemble the Five-spotted Moth, and are only distinguished by characters which would not be noticed except by the entomologist.

Many devices have been resorted to in order to lessen the number and mitigate the ravages of the Tobacco-worm, but the lack of general and continued efforts from year to year has brought only partial relief. Some years they come in great numbers, and despite the best efforts of the planter, seriously damage his crop. Perhaps the next year, they are few, and give him no trouble. It is the nature of this insect to raise at least two broods during the year. The hawk-moth or tobacco-fly usually makes its appearance in Virginia in the month of May. The eggs, deposited by the first moths, hatch out in from five to seven days, larvæ or worms. The worm sheds its outer skin twice before it gets its growth. The growing stage of the worm lasts from twenty-five to thirty days, and after it has attained its growth, it gorges itself a few days longer, and then crawls or burrows into the ground, where it soon passes into the pupa state; and after some twenty-three or twenty-five days from the time of its crawling into the ground the pupa sends forth a moth to lay more eggs and hatch out more worms. Each moth is capable of laying on an average two hundred eggs. So that for every moth in May we may reasonably expect at least one hundred worms of the first brood; and if none of these are destroyed, but all allowed to change to moths, and these latter to raise a horde of worms, what wonder that the second brood sometimes appears in such countless numbers as to defy all efforts to destroy them before they have ruined the crop? Every moth ought to be destroyed as they appear; this may be done to great extent by injecting a few drops of sweetened Cobalts into the flowers of the Petunia, if growing near, which will give them their final quietus.

At present this pest appears to be unknown in England, and it is to be hoped that our climate will not be found acceptable to its tastes and development.

A USEFUL TOBACCO BARN.

Size: Length, 30 feet; width, 20 feet; height to plating or bottom of ridge, 27 feet, including 18 inches brickwork, as shown here.* Capacity, to hold one acre of Tobacco.

It will be observed that the Barn as illustrated here, which is highly recommended in America, has portable sides, the object of these being to admit as much light and air as possible during bright, dry weather.

ENGLISH TOBACCO CULTURE A HUNDRED YEARS AGO,

BEING

INSTRUCTIONS FOR CULTIVATING AND CURING TOBACCO.

FROM MR. CARVER'S TREATISE ON THAT SUBJECT.

Extracted from the Annual Register; or, A View of the History of Politics and Literature. For the Year 1779. Printed for J. Dodsley, in Pall Mall, 1796.

THE best ground for raising the plant is a warm, rich soil, not subject to be overrun with weeds, for from these it must be totally cleared. The soil in which it grows in Virginia is inclining to sandy, consequently warm and light; the nearer, therefore, the nature of the land approaches to that, the greater probability there is of its flourishing here. The situation most preferable for a plantation is the southern declivity of a hill, or a spot that is sheltered from the blighting north winds which so frequently blow during the spring months in this island. But at the same time the plants must enjoy a free current of air; for if that be obstructed, they will not prosper.

As the Tobacco plant, being an annual, is only to be raised from seed, the greatest care in purchasing these is necessary, lest by sowing such as is not good, we lose with the expected crop the season. The different sorts of the seeds not being distinguishable from each other, nor the goodness to be ascertained by their appearance, the purchaser should apply to a person of character in that profession. In describing the manner in which the plant ought to be raised from the seed, as well as in succeeding progress, I shall confine myself to the practice of the northern colonies of America, as these are more parallel in their latitude to England.

About the middle of April, or rather sooner in a forward spring, sow the seed in beds, first prepared for the purpose with some warm rich manure. In a cold spring, regular hotbeds would be most eligible for this purpose, and indeed the gardeners of this country are persuaded that the Nicotiana cannot be raised in any other way; but these are seldom to be found in common gardens, and I am convinced that if the weather is not remarkably severe, they might be reared without doors. A square yard of land, for which a small quantity of seed is sufficient, will produce above five hundred plants, and allow proper space for their nurture till they are fit to transplant.

Having sown the seed in the manner directed, on the least apprehension of a frost after the plants appear, it will be necessary to spread mats over the beds, elevated from the ground by poles laid across. These, however, must be removed in the morning soon after the sun appears, that they may receive as much benefit as possible from its warmth, and from the air. In this manner proceed till the leaves have attained the size of about two inches in length, and one in breadth, which they will do in about a month, or near the middle of May. One invariable rule for their being able to bear removal, is when the fourth leaf is sprouted, and the fifth just appears. Then take the opportunity of the first rains or gentle showers to transplant them into such a soil and situation as before described. The land must be ploughed or dug up with spades, as mellow and light as possible. Raise with the hoe small hillocks at the distance of two feet or a little more from each other, taking care that no hard sods or lumps are in them, and then just indent the middle of each, without dibbling the holes as for some other plants. When your ground is thus prepared, dig up the plants in a gentle manner from their native bed, and insert a plant gently into the centre of each hillock, pressing the soil around it with your fingers, and taking the greatest care during the operation that you do not break off any of the leaves, which are at this time exquisitely tender. If the weather proves dry after they are thus transplanted, they must be watered with soft water in the same manner as is usually done to coleworts, or plants of a similar kind. From this time great care must be taken to keep the ground soft and free from weeds, by often stirring with your hoe the mould round the roots, and pruning off the dead leaves that sometimes are found near the bottom of the stalk. The difference of this climate from that in which I have been accustomed to observe the progress of this plant, will not permit me to direct with certainty the time which is most proper to take off the top of it to prevent it from running to seed. This knowledge can only be perfectly acquired by experience. When it has risen to upwards of two feet, it commonly begins to put forth the branches on which the flowers and seeds are produced; but as this expansion, if suffered to take place, would drain the nutriment from the leaves, and thereby lessen their size and efficacy, it becomes needful at this stage to nip off the extremity of the stalk to prevent its growing higher. In some higher climates, the top is commonly cut off when the plant has fifteen leaves; if the Tobacco is intended to be a little stronger, this is done when it has only thirteen; and sometimes when it is chosen to be remarkably powerful, eleven or twelve leaves only are allowed to expand. On the contrary, if the planter is desirous to have his crop very mild, he suffers it to put forth eighteen or twenty; but in this calculation the three or four lower leaves next the ground are not to be reckoned.

This is denominated "topping the Tobacco," and is much better done by finger and thumb than with any instrument, because the former close at the same time the pores of the plants, whereas, when it is done with the latter, the juices are in some degree exhausted. And though this might appear unimportant, yet every method that tends to give vigour to the leaves should be carefully pursued. For the same reason, care must be taken to nip off the sprouts that will be continually springing up at the junction of the leaves with the stalks. This is termed "suckering the Tobacco," and ought to be repeated as often as occasion requires.

The last, and not the least, concern in the cultivation of this plant, is the destruction of the worm that Nature has given it for an enemy, and which, like many other reptiles, plays on its benefactor. To destroy these, which are the only insects that molest this plant, every leaf must be carefully searched. As soon as such a wound is discovered, the cause of it, from his unsubstantial texture, which I shall frequently describe, may be easily crushed; but the best method is to pluck it away by the horn and then crush it. Without a constant attention to these noxious insects, a whole field of plants may be soon destroyed. This is termed "worming the Tobacco," and as these worms are found most predominant the latter end of July and the beginning of August, they must be particularly attended to at that season.

As I have just observed that it is impossible, without experience, to point out the due time for topping the plant, so it is equally as impossible to ascertain the time it will take to ripen in this climate. That can only be known by future observations; for as it is at present only cultivated in England as an ornament for the garden, no particular attention has, I believe, been hitherto bestowed on the preservation of its leaves. The apparent signs, however, of its maturity are, that the leaves, as they approach a state of ripeness, become more corrugated or rough, and, when fully ripe, appear mottled with yellowish spots on the raised parts, whilst the cavities retain their usual green colour. They are at this time also thicker than they have before been, and are covered with a kind of downy velvet. If heavy rains happen at this critical period, they will wash this excrescent substance off, and thereby damage the plants. In such a case, if the frosty nights are not begun, it is proper to let them stand a few days longer, when, if the weather be more moderate, they will recover this substance again. But if a frost unexpectedly happens during the night, they must be carefully examined in the morning before the sun has any influence on them, and those which are found to be covered with frosty particles, whether thoroughly ripe or not, must be cut up, and though they may not all appear to be arrived at a state of maturity, yet they cannot be far from it, and will differ but little in goodness from those that are perfectly so.

Having now given every instruction that occurs to my memory relative to the culture of the plant, I shall describe the worm that infects it. It is of the horned species, and appears to be peculiar to this plant; so that in many parts of America it is distinguished by the name of the Tobacco-worm. The first time it is discernible is when the plants have gained about half their height; it then appears to be nearly as large as a gnat; soon after which it lengthens into a worm, and by degrees increases to the size of a man's finger. In shape it is regular from its head to its tail, without any diminution at either extremity, indented or ribbed round at equal distances nearly a quarter of an inch from each other, and having at every one of these divisions a pair of claws by which it fastens itself to the plant. Its mouth, like that of the caterpillar, is placed under the forepart of the head. On the top of the body grows a horn about half an inch in length, and greatly resembling a thorn, the extreme part of which is brown, of a firm texture, and sharp-pointed. By this horn, as before observed, it is usually plucked from the leaf.

When the plant is fit for gathering, on the first morning that promises a fair day, before the sun is risen, take a long knife, and holding the stalk near the top with one hand, sever it from its root with the other as low as possible. Having done this, lay it gently on the ground, and there let it remain exposed to the sun throughout the day, or until the leaves are entirely wilted, as it is termed in America; that is, till they become limber, and will bend any way without breaking. If, on the contrary, the rain should continue without any intervals, and the plant appears to be full ripe, they must be cut down and housed immediately. This must be done, however, with great care that the leaves, which are in this state very brittle, may not be broken. Being placed under proper shelter, either in a barn or a covered hovel, where they cannot be affected by the rain or too much air, they must be thinly scattered on the floor: and if the sun does not appear for several days, so that they can be laid out again, they must remain to wilt in that manner, which is not indeed so desirable as in the sun, nor will the tobacco prove quite so good. When the leaves have acquired the flexibility before described, the plants must be laid in heaps, or rather in one heap, if the quantity be not too great, and in about twenty-four hours they will be found to sweat. But during this time, when they have lain for a little while, and begin to ferment, it is necessary to turn them, that the whole quantity may be equally fermented. The longer they lie in this situation, the darker-coloured the Tobacco becomes. This is termed "sweating the Tobacco."

After they have lain in this manner for three or four days, for in a longer time they grow mouldy, the plants may be tied together in pairs, and hung across a pole in the same covered place, a proper interval being left between each pair. In about a month they will be thoroughly dried, and of a proper temperature to be taken down. This state may be ascertained by their appearing of the same colour as those imported from America, with which few are unacquainted. But this can be done at no other season than during wet weather; for the Tobacco abounding with salts, it is always affected if there is the least humidity in the atmosphere, even though it be hung in a dry place. If this rule be not observed, but they are removed in dry weather, the leaves will crumble, and a considerable waste will attend its removal.

As soon as the plants are taken down, they must once more be laid in a heap, and pressed with heavy logs of wood for about a week. This climate, however, may require a longer time. Whilst they remain in this state, it will be necessary to introduce your hand frequently into the heap, to discover whether the heat be too intense; for in large quantities this will sometimes be the case, and considerable damage will accrue from it. When the heat exceeds a moderate glowing warmth, part of the weight by which they are compressed must be taken away, and the cause being removed, the effect will cease. This is called "the second or last sweating," and when completed, which it generally will be in about the time just mentioned, the leaves may be stripped from the stalks for use. Many omit this last operation, but it takes away any remaining hardness, and renders the Tobacco more mellow. When the leaves are stripped from the stalks, they are to be tied up in bunches, and kept in a cellar, or any other place that is damp; though if not handled in dry weather, but only during a rainy season, it is of little consequence in what part of the house or barn they are laid up. At this period the Tobacco is thoroughly cured, and equally proper for manufacturing as that imported from the Colonies. If it has been properly managed that raw fiery taste so commonly found in the common sale Tobacco will be totally eradicated, and though it retains all its strength, will be soft and pleasing in its flavour. Those who are curious in their Tobacco in the Northern Colonies of America sprinkle it, when made up into rolls for keeping, with small common white wines or cyder, instead of salt water, which gives it an inexpressibly fine flavour.

By pursuing the rules which I have endeavoured to give in as explicit terms as possible, country gentlemen, and landholders in general, will be enabled to raise much better Tobacco than that which is usually imported from Maryland and Virginia; for notwithstanding there are not wanting prohibitory laws in those countries, to prevent the planters from sending to market any but the principal leaves, yet they frequently, to increase their profit, suffer the sprouts to grow and mix the smaller leaves of these with the others, which renders them much inferior in goodness.

The crops that I have reason to believe may be raised in England, will greatly exceed in flavour and efficacy any that is imported from the Southern Colonies, for though Northern climates require far more care and exactness to bring Tobacco to a proper state of maturity than warmer latitudes, yet this tardiness of growth tends to impregnate the plant with a greater quantity of salts, and consequently with that aromatic flavour for which it is prized, than is to be found in the produce of hotter climes, where it is brought to a state of perfection from the seed, in half the time required in colder regions.

A pound of Tobacco raised in New England or Nova Scotia, is supposed to contain as much real strength as two pounds from Virginia, and I doubt not but that near double the quantity of salts might be extracted from it by chemical process.

I shall also just add, though the example can only be followed in particular parts of these kingdoms, that the Americans usually choose for the place where they intend to make the seedling-bed, part of a copse, or a spot of ground covered with wood, of which they burn down such a portion as they think necessary. Having done this, they rake up the subjacent mould, and mixing it with the ashes thus produced, sow therein the seed, without adding any other manure, or taking any other steps. Where this method cannot be pursued, wood-ashes may be strewed over the mould in which the seed is designed to be sown.

To the uses already known, there is another to which Tobacco might be applied, that I believe has never been thought of by Europeans; and which may render it much more estimable than any other. It has been found by the Americans to answer the purpose of tanning leather, as well, if not better, than bark; and was not the latter so plentiful in their country, would be generally used by them instead of it. I have been witness to many experiments wherein it has proved successful, especially on the thinner sorts of hides, and can safely pronounce it to be, in countries where bark is scarce, a valuable substitute for that article.

TOBACCO IN NEW ZEALAND.

TOBACCO GROWN IN TAURANGA.—"A resident in this town has sent to our office some magnificent samples of Tobacco grown by himself. He has sent us both the green leaf and the dried, and as specimens they are unique and well worthy of inspection. There are four samples. No. 1 is the *Nicotiana rustica*, or what is known as Turkish Tobacco; the leaf measures 19 inches long by 12 inches wide. No. 2 is the *Nicotiana tabacina*, or the Virginian leaf, and measures 32 inches by 10 inches, and is used for Cake Tobacco. No. 3 sample is the Virginian leaf used for cigar wraps, and measures 33 inches by 13 inches. No. 4 is the Native, or Maori leaf, and measures 13 inches by 4 inches. The seed was obtained from an American gentleman resident in Virginia, who had visited New Zealand to ascertain whether Tobacco could be successfully grown in this country, and if these specimens are to be taken as a criterion, it may safely be asserted that the matter is settled, for these leaves are fit to bear any scrutiny. The gentleman who sent us the samples as evidence of his successful cultivation, hopes to see this industry followed out, and tells us. that he is willing to take the oversight of the cultivation and curing, free of charge, for any person who will be willing to grow, say, from two to three acres of leaf. The land chosen must be good ground, and sloping with right aspect, so as to have a protection from the north-west wind. The plants from which the leaves were taken yielded in some instances as many as twenty-eight of these magnificent leaves. We invite an inspection of these samples."
—*New Zealand Paper.*

TOBACCO IN GERMANY.

The chief producer of Tobacco is, as is well known, its home, America, whose power of producing is not nearly approached by that of any other division of the earth. The further, however, the love of Tobacco spread outside America, the more the cultivation of it also increased outside that country. The smoking nations of this quarter of the globe do their utmost, and very justifiably too, to provide for their own needs as far as possible; unfortunately, the results do not always correspond to their exertions—at least, as far as flavour is concerned.

In Europe the best cigars are produced by Turkey, Russia, Hungary, Germany, and France, but they are far surpassed by the United States of America, Cuba, and Brazil. Germany and France are even behind Japan, Peru, and China.

In spite of that, the cultivation of Tobacco in Germany is more important than is generally believed. The area of the ground grown with Tobacco amounted to 21,800 hectares; the yield of the cured leaves (taking the average of the last two years) to 41,728 tons. But this is not nearly enough for the requirements of the home Tobacco industry in raw Tobacco. About 40 per cent. of the quantity used is imported. The imports of raw Tobacco leaves and shavings Tobacco stems exceeded the exports every year (taking the average of the last six years) by 27,583 tons, amounting in value to 45,428,000 marks.

These numbers speak clearly for the enormous importance of the Tobacco industry, in which, according to the statistics of the 5th of June, 1882, 110,468 persons were occupied solely with carrying it on; of these, 62,933 were of the male, and 47,535 of the female, sex.

It would be interesting to know exactly from what countries, and in what quantities from each of them, Germany draws its Tobacco. This information cannot be obtained from the imperial statistics, as, in consequence of Hamburg and Bremen being free ports, all goods imported through these towns are put down to their account, and all those coming *viâ* English and Dutch ports to their account. Europe, chiefly from North America, the West Indies, Java, Sumatra, Columbia, Venezuela, etc.— *Tabak Zeitung.*

TOBACCO IN FRANCE.

While the quantity of Tobacco grown in France was about 19,200 tons in 1850, it has been gradually increasing until it is now nearly double that quantity, while the revenue which the State derives from it has increased from £3,555,000 to nearly £13,000,000. In other words, while the quantity of Tobacco grown has only doubled, the profits of the State, or in other words of the manufacturers, have nearly quadrupled. The great increase in profit is explained upon the ground that the expense of manufacturing an additional quantity of Tobacco is not anything like that of the first establishment of plant and material. The cultivation and manufacture of Tobacco has been a Government monopoly since 1674, and, with the exception of a brief interval during the Revolution, has remained so ever since. The following figures show the quantity of Tobacco consumed in the different countries of Europe, and the rate per 100 inhabitants is as follows:—Spain, 110 lbs.; Italy, 128 lbs.; Great Britain, 138 lbs.; Russia, 182 lbs.; Hungary, 207 lbs.; France, 210 lbs.; Denmark, 224 lbs.; Norway, 229 lbs.; Austria, 273 lbs.; Germany, 336 lbs.; Holland, 448 lbs.; and Belgium, 560 lbs. In other words, while in Spain little more than one pound per head is consumed, nearly double that quantity is consumed in France, three times as much in Germany, four times as much in Holland, and five times as much in Berlin.—*Tobacco.*

TOBACCO IN THE UNITED STATES.

Whilst John Bull is thinking about trying to grow his own Tobacco, Uncle Sam is making an attempt to grow more than he does now. The last monthly report of the Department of Agriculture for the State of Carolina (U.S.A.) announces that, in order to practically test Tobacco-growing in South Carolina, and to ascertain whether it can be made a profitable crop, the Board of Agriculture has appropriated £360 to encourage experiments by farmers in the State. The Department has selected one farmer in each county to experiment in the cultivation of Tobacco, and will pay the sum of £10 to each farmer appointed for this purpose; and this sum will be paid after the crop has been cured and ready for market, and samples, with reports prescribed, have been sent to the Commissioner of Agriculture, provided all the requirements made by the Department have been complied with. The Board of Agriculture has also appropriated £20 as a premium to the farmer reporting the best results in the growing of Tobacco for the season 1886. This premium is open to any farmer in the State who desires to contest for it, and who will follow the rules of the Department governing the contest. The farmers selected in each county by the Department to make the experiments, and all others who desire to compete for the £20 premium, will be required to send a statement of the average temperature of the weather (compiled from daily record) and the condition of the crop to the Commissioner of Agriculture on the first of each month, and to send a sample of the Tobacco, when cured, to the Department of Agriculture, weighing not less than 10 lbs. The £20 premium will be awarded by the Board of Agriculture after all the reports of results and the samples have been received.—*Tobacco.*

TOBACCO IN AUSTRALIA.

In this connection it may be worth while to mention that Tobacco cultivation in Australia, especially in New South Wales, has proved an unmistakable success. In that colony last year about 1,603 acres were devoted to growing Tobacco, the quantity obtained being 12,947 cwts. The leaf is of excellent quality, equal to any obtained from Cuba or Manila. It is retained principally for home consumption, being readily purchased by local manufacturers.—*Tobacco*.

TOBACCO IN SPAIN.

The annual consumption of Tobacco is in Spain at an average rate of 48 kilograms for every 100 persons; in Italy, 58; in England, 63; in Russia, 84; in France, 96; in Norway, 104; in Denmark, 106; in Austria, 127; in Germany, 152; in Holland, 203; and in Belgium 246. The kilogram equals two pounds avoirdupois.--*Tobacco*.

TOBACCO AMONGST THE AMERICAN INDIANS.

The Susquehannah Indians, when addressed by some Christian missionaries on the origin of all things, gave them, in turn, the origin of Tobacco to the following effect :—" Some hunters of their tribe having killed and cooked a deer, observed the figure like that of a young woman—really a spirit—on the hill-side, and thinking that she might be suffering from hunger, offered her some venison. She partook of it, and was pleased with its flavour, and said : 'Your kindness shall be rewarded ; come here thirteen moons hence, and you shall find it.' They did so ; and found maize growing where her right hand had touched the ground ; where her left, kidney beans ; and where she had sat they found *Tobacco*."—*Tobacco Whiffs*.

USEFUL HINTS

CULLED FROM

THE BRAINS OF AMERICAN CULTIVATORS.

OPEN AIR BEDS.—There is no question but that open air beds are cheapest. And, where this mode of raising plants is practicable, it is greatly to be preferred for the main supply of plants. It is a well-established opinion that plants raised in the open air stand transplanting better and usually grow off quicker than plants raised in hotbed or cold frame.

SELECTION OF SOIL, PREPARATION AND MANURING.—The Tobacco plant thrives best in a deep, mellow, loamy soil, rich or made so with manures. The subsoil ought to be sufficiently porous to permit the water falling on the surface to pass downward readily, and not to accumulate to drown and stagnate.

If old land is selected, it ought to be fallowed deep in the fall or early winter, that the frosts may pulverise it. Turn under, if possible, some coarse farm manure, for its decay will greatly help to loosen the soil, while furnishing pabulum for the crop. As a coarse manure for yellow Tobacco, nothing is better than wheat straw turned under in the fall and winter. The plants rarely fail to ripen yellow in colour on land thus treated.

In the early spring more manure may be applied, but it is better that this should come from the compost heap. Follow the application of the compost with one-horse turning ploughs, *crossing* the previous ploughing, turning not exceeding four or five inches deep—about half the depth of the first ploughing. Then, just before it is time to plant, run double-shovel ploughs over the lot, *crossing* the previous furrows, and follow with harrow or drag, *crossing* again to thoroughly make fine. These repeated ploughings, *crossing each time every previous one*, never fail, if the work is done when the land is in proper condition, to put it in proper tilth.

Let the planter remember that "a good preparation is half cultivation," and not stop till the land is in proper condition.

Never "scrape down" Tobacco with the hoe without putting back on hill or bed as much dirt as is scraped down. This will prevent baking, and save many plants, should a dry spell follow the hand-hoe working.

Any process which stirs the soil effectually and often, and keeps the plants free from grass and weeds, will constitute good cultivation, no matter how or with what implement done. Old land will require more work in cultivation than new, and dark grades more than bright. Short single trees should be used after the plants are half-grown, to prevent tearing and breaking the leaves.

STRIPPING.—Tobacco should never be stripped from the stalks except in pliable order, and the leaves on every plant should be carefully assorted and every grade tied up separately. Usually there will be three grades of leaf, assorted with reference to colour and size, and two of lugs. If bulked down, watch frequently to see that it does not heat. If the bulk becomes warm it must be broken up, aired and rebulked, or hung up if too soft.

CHARLES DICKENS AND EVANS, PRINTERS, CRYSTAL PALACE.

SPECIAL NOTICE.—*The price of the "Gardeners' Chronicle" is now reduced to* THREEPENCE.

"First to our hand come the home journals, among which the ably conducted 'Gardeners' Chronicle' worthily holds the lead, as it has now done for more than a generation."—*The Journal of Forestry.*

"Energetic, yet conservative, the 'Gardeners' Chronicle' has become useful and popular everywhere."
HON. MARSHALL WILDER, Boston, U.S.

"Forgive me if I pay a compliment to the way the 'Chronicle' is edited. It is ab y and well managed."—*An Orchidist.*

THE
Gardeners' Chronicle

("THE TIMES" OF HORTICULTURE.)

A WEEKLY ILLUSTRATED JOURNAL,

(*Established* 1841.)

Every Friday, price THREEPENCE ; *post free*, THREEPENCE-HALFPENNY.

THE "GARDENERS' CHRONICLE" has been for nearly fifty years the leading journal of its class.

It has achieved this position because, while specially devoting itself to supplying the daily requirements of Gardeners of all classes, much of the information furnished is of such general and *permanent value*, that the "Gardeners' Chronicle" is looked up to as the *standard authority* on the subjects on which it treats.

CIRCULATION.—Its relations with Amateur and Professional Gardeners and with the Horticultural Trade of all countries, are of a specially extensive character.

CONTRIBUTORS.—Its contributors comprise the leading British Gardeners and many of the most eminent men of science at home and abroad.

ILLUSTRATIONS.—The "Gardeners' Chronicle" has obtained an international reputation for the accuracy, permanent utility, and artistic effect of its illustrations of plants. These illustrations, together with the original articles and monographs, render the "Gardeners' Chronicle" an indispensable work of reference in all garden reading-rooms and botanical libraries.

SUPPLEMENTS.—Double-page engravings, lithographs, and other illustrations of large size, are frequently given as Supplements, without extra charge.

ALL SUBSCRIPTIONS PAYABLE IN ADVANCE.

THE UNITED KINGDOM—Twelve Months, **15s.**; Six Months, **7s. 6d.**; Three Months, **3s. 9d.**; Post Free. FOREIGN SUBSCRIPTIONS (EXCEPTING INDIA AND CHINA)—Including Postage, **17s. 6d.** for Twelve Months; India and China, **19s. 6d.**

P.O.O. to be made payable at the Post Office, No. 42, DRURY LANE, London, to W. RICHARDS. Cheques should be crossed "DRUMMOND."

Telegraphic Address—GARDCHRON, LONDON.

Office: 41, WELLINGTON ST., STRAND, LONDON, W.C.

The Gardening World

SUPPLIES A WANT OF THE AGE.

A First-Class Gardening Paper for One Penny.

UNIVERSALLY ADMITTED TO BE
THE CHEAPEST AND BEST GARDENERS' WEEKLY NEWSPAPER.

THE GARDENING WORLD is published every Friday morning, and can be obtained through all Newsagents and Booksellers, and from all Railway Bookstalls, or sent direct from the Office for 6s. 6d. per annum, prepaid. Foreign Subscription to all Countries in the Postal Union, 8s. 8d. Vols. I. and II., handsomely bound, 6s. 6d. each.

A SPECIMEN COPY SENT FREE TO ANY ADDRESS.

Postal and Money Orders should be made payable to B. WYNNE, at Drury Lane.

PUBLISHING OFFICE:
17, Catherine Street, Covent Garden, London, W.C.

THE BEST MONDAY AGRICULTURAL JOURNAL.

The AGRICULTURAL GAZETTE
(ESTABLISHED 1844),
FOR LANDHOLDERS AND TENANT FARMERS.
Every Monday, price 4d.; post free, 4½d.

The "AGRICULTURAL GAZETTE" gives Full Market Reports, both Metropolitan and Provincial; accurate Accounts of Prices and Sales, Proceedings of Agricultural Societies, Farmers' Clubs, and Chambers of Agriculture—their Meetings, Exhibitions, and Discussions are reported fully, and with promptitude.

Especial attention is given to Agricultural Implement Manufacture.
NO EXPENSE IS SPARED IN ILLUSTRATIONS.

Not only Implements, but Plants, Weeds, varieties of Cultivated Crops, etc.; and Animals—Breeds of Horses, Cattle, Sheep, and Pigs; also Poultry, Insects, General Natural History; and Buildings—Farmhouses, Homesteads, Cottages; Photographs illustrative of Country Life and Occupations, whether at Home or Abroad—all these provide subjects for the Engraver.

PORTRAITS and MEMOIRS of NOTEWORTHY AGRICULTURISTS are also occasionally given.

SUBSCRIPTIONS PAYABLE IN ADVANCE,
Including Postage to any part of the United Kingdom:

Twelve Months, 19s. 6d.; Six Months, 9s. 9d.; Three Months, 5s.
P.O.O. to be made payable at the King Street Post Office, W.C., to ALEXANDER K. BRUCE.

PUBLISHING OFFICE AND OFFICE FOR ADVERTISEMENTS:
9, NEW BRIDGE ST., LUDGATE CIRCUS, E.C.

THE
Journal of Horticulture

COTTAGE GARDENER and HOME FARMER.

Conducted by ROBERT HOGG, LL.D., F.L.S.

Assisted by a Staff of the Best Writers on Practical Gardening, and numerous Amateur and Professional Writers eminent in the various Departments of Horticulture and other Rural Pursuits connected with the Household.

It has been established for a period of nearly FORTY YEARS, and has long been regarded as the

LEADING JOURNAL OF PRACTICAL HORTICULTURE.

This widely-circulating Journal consists of Thirty-two Pages of Letterpress, with occasional Supplements, and is richly Illustrated with Wood Engravings in the highest style of the Art.

The JOURNAL OF HORTICULTURE contains the Earliest Reports of all the Important Horticultural and other Shows.

GARDENING in all its aspects is treated exhaustively by the most practical and successful Cultivators of the day.

HOME FARM.—This Department contains sound and seasonable advice on Profitable Cropping, Stock Management, Manures and their application, and the most approved Modes of Dairy Farming.

BEES.—The most advanced Apiarians and the most successful Bee-keepers in Great Britain are contributors to this section of this long-established and increasingly-popular Publication.

A NEW VOLUME COMMENCES THE FIRST WEEK IN JANUARY.

Published Weekly, price 3d.; Post Free, 3½d.

TERMS OF SUBSCRIPTION:
One Quarter, 3s. 9d.; Half Year, 7s. 6d; One Year, 15s.
P.O.O.'s to be made payable to EDWARD H. MAY.

TO BE HAD OF ALL BOOKSELLERS & RAILWAY BOOKSTALLS.

OFFICE:
171, FLEET STREET, LONDON, E.C.

CARTERS'
"FIRST ENGLISH"
(Registered Trade Mark.)
TOBACCO.

Awarded the Silver Banksian Medal, R.H.S., 1886.

The first and only Award ever made to English-grown Tobacco.

In this Catalogue we offer Seeds of a great variety of Tobacco, those sorts marked thus *, we have proved to be most distinct in character and ornamental in appearance.

Specimen Plants of Tobacco form noble Botanical objects, and no garden is complete without them.

Full instructions for Cultivation accompany every packet of Seed.

TOBACCO SEED.

	Price per packet—s. d. s. d.		Price per packet—s. d. s. d.
*Big Frederick, deep green	1 0 & 2 6	*Kentucky, golden-green foliage	1 0 & 2 6
*Yellow Prior, fine rich green	1 0 ,, 2 6	Maryland Broadleaf, pale green	1 0 ,, 2 6
*Connecticut, fine green	1 0 ,, 2 6	*Pennsylvania, pale green	1 0 ,, 2 6
*White Burleigh, very distinct	1 0 ,, 2 6	Mixed Varieties	— 2 6

Many of the following varieties are offered this Season for the first time—

Havana.	Big Orinoco.	Turkish Bostea.
Seedleaf.	Big Havana.	Turkish Latakieh.
Florida.	Stirling.	Turkish Salonicke.
Hester Virginia.	Hopgood.	Stockholm.
*One Sucker.	Flanagan.	Hungarian Carlusk.
Virginia.	Tuckahoe.	Hungarian Debroc.
Island Broadleaf.	James River.	Hungarian St. Andras.
White Stem.	Raffleleaf.	Hungarian Verpelet.
*Yellow Orinoco.	Missouri.	Hungarian Muscat.
Glasner.	Ohio.	Hungarian Galois.
General Grant.	Hyco.	

Each, price per packet, 1/- and 2/6.

"During the past week we have had in this country the novel sight of a tobacco harvest, and it is extremely probable that in one or two churches this year plants and flowers of Nicotiana will blend with grapes, fruits, wheats, and vegetables in their silent homage of Harvest Thanksgiving. The harvest has been gathered in in some dozen parts of England, **Messrs. Carters' Crop at Holloway Farm, Bromley, of course, leading the way, this firm having imported the Seed for nearly all, if not all, the trial crops.**"—*Morning Post.*

Seedsmen by Royal Warrants to H.M. The Queen,
and H.R.H. The Prince of Wales,

237 & 238, HIGH HOLBORN, LONDON.

www.ingramcontent.com/pod-product-compliance
Lightning Source LLC
Chambersburg PA
CBHW020106170426
43199CB00009B/413